Midlife Battle Cry

Midlife Battle Cry

REDEFINING THE
MIGHTY SECOND HALF

DAWN BARTON

W Publishing Group

An Imprint of Thomas Nelson

© 2023 W Publishing

Published in Nashville, Tennessee, by W Publishing, an imprint of Thomas Nelson.

Thomas Nelson titles may be purchased in bulk for educational, business, fundraising, or sales promotional use. For information, please email SpecialMarkets@ThomasNelson.com.

Unless otherwise noted, Scripture quotations are taken from the Holy Bible, New Living Translation. © 1996, 2004, 2015 by Tyndale House Foundation. Used by permission of Tyndale House Publishers, Inc., Carol Stream, Illinois 60188. All rights reserved.

Any internet addresses, phone numbers, or company or product information printed in this book are offered as a resource and are not intended in any way to be or to imply an endorsement by Thomas Nelson, nor does Thomas Nelson vouch for the existence, content, or services of these sites, phone numbers, companies, or products beyond the life of this book.

ISBN 978-0-7852-9484-9 (audiobook)
ISBN 978-0-7852-9483-2 (eBook)
ISBN 978-0-7852-9482-5 (TP)

Library of Congress Control Number: 2022051924

Printed in the United States of America
23 24 25 26 27 LBC 5 4 3 2 1

For Mom and Dad
Thank you for showing me what it is to fully
love and live in every season of life.

Contents

CONTENTS

Read This First

I left it all: the job, the accolades, the paycheck. Even the free fancy car. It was 2018, and I was following a God calling. I was certain my life would change dramatically over the next six months. I was about to become a best-selling author embarking on my glamorous book tour with audiences that I just knew would rival the attendance of any Adele concert. My future was bright, and I was ready to step into all that it had for me. After all, I had been obediently following that God calling. Surely, God would not call me to write a book and not make that book the single most transcendent publication of the twenty-first century.

As you may have surmised, I have a very creative—dare I say, ridiculous—imagination on occasion. The reality of how this famous author fantasy played out was a wee bit different. It took over two years for *Laughing Through the Ugly Cry* to come out, and that baby released smack-dab in the middle of a global pandemic, throwing a big sweaty mask over my dreams of stadium-only book signings and TV morning show interviews.

Worst of all, somewhere amid the reality of leaving a big career with a handsome paycheck, navigating the endless book-publishing process, and, well, trying to stay healthy during a pandemic, a certain number appeared above my head, hovering there like a massive, sad cloud. 50. *You are turning 50*, it said, *and you are done.*

I'd always assumed that by the time I hit half a century in age or, as I like to call it, *fiddy*, I'd be in the best physical shape of my life. (Oprah did this, so I assumed it was just part of the fifty package. It's not.) I believed I would have accomplished enormous, momentous things, the least of which was changing the world. My reality was *not* how it was supposed to play out.

As my birthday came and went, I found I was struggling with my identity and my purpose. I was flailing. I wondered if this was what they call a "midlife crisis"—but that seemed a tad inadequate. This new season felt more like an end-of-life, end-of-a-working-metabolism, end-of-sleeping-through-the-night great wall of depression, rather than a temporary crisis.

The general idea is that when men go through a midlife crisis, they buy fancy red sports cars or ridiculously oversized Ford 250 Super Duty trucks with a towing capacity of twenty-three million pounds—because you just never know when you might need to tow your M1 Abrams tank out to the hunting camp.

When women go through it, we stare into mirrors, asking ourselves if our skin is actually melting and sliding off our bodies and, if so, how much farther can it possibly slide? We obsess over all the things we didn't do, all the places we never saw, how much therapy our children will need after their time with us, why we never took up salsa dancing, and whether we will wake up one day and just be bones and muscles because, seriously, our skin has literally slid down and gathered at our ankles. Suddenly, a man's plan to take out a third mortgage so he can tow a tank seems so much more reasonable than this deep emotional dive.

The truth is I was not exiting my forties gracefully. I was lost and behaving like an emotional, hormonal high school girl. It felt like there was only one thing to do—throw a long, extravagant, I'm-fifty-and-life-is-over pity party. A Scarlett O'Hara pity party where I flung my body on the sofa with the back of my hand against my forehead in dramatic fashion. An overblown, Southern pity party. The best kind.

But my party wasn't fun. It was a slow-moving hurricane of negative emotions and lies that shouted, "The world is done with you! You are too old, you are not relevant anymore, and you are definitely not cool." (I think we all know that last one is straight from the devil himself because, if I am anything, it is *cool*. Just ask my teenager.) I felt like I had become a used-up old racehorse, and the world was putting this old mare out to pasture.

Now, I may not be the sharpest tool in the shed, but I know this: pity parties are complete downers, and people rarely attend them. There comes a time when you have to get up, lace up those tennis shoes with your snazzy orthopedic inserts, and figure it out. I needed to change my mindset and quit feeling like a victim of Father Time. I was fifty, but was that a bad thing? Was it really the beginning of the end, or perhaps just the kickoff of the mighty second half?

I took time to do a slow internal audit, and I realized something: I really like who I am. Are there things I wish were different? Of course. Should I exercise more, eat better, and volunteer at my child's school for the first time? Absolutely. Am I going to? Probably not, and that's okay.

I made a conscious choice right then to make changes and view things in a new way. I decided I will live boldly, embracing all that makes me the woman I am today. I refuse to be a spectator of life. Instead, I will be a wild participant, because life is for the living. I want to be used every day, like an old Bible. A worn, weathered old Bible representing a life with marked pages, tear stains, and blessings. I'm going to soak it all up—the people, the lessons, the time. The world will know I was here.

The truth is, our "midlife" is just a pivot point, and it's not determined by a particular number. It's a season, a change, and an awakening. God doesn't bring us to the middle of our lives and say, "Thanks so much for your service. We had a terrific run. Now, watch some Netflix, and I'll call you when your time is up." There is no "midlife" to God. We are His gift to this world at every age and every season. But I believe that THIS season and THIS age are the best yet.

In the second half of life, we are more ourselves than we have ever been. For many of you reading, your children have left the nest; for those of you who never had kids, people have finally stopped asking you why. You understand that your self-worth isn't wrapped up in an accolade from work, nor is it defined by the decor of your home and your culinary skills. Maybe you left a bad marriage and are regaining your footing, maybe your second marriage is finally hitting the comfort zone, or maybe you've been married thirty years and can happily pass gas in bed now. Maybe you never married, and gosh darn it, you're proud of it. You're not forty trying to look thirty; you're where you are. You have the confidence to say no to the mundane and yes to the new.

Yes to the challenging, the exciting, the scary, the ridiculous, and the meaningful. To all that you haven't let yourself even consider for so long.

Right now, right here is our sweet spot. It's the crossroads of age and experience, and it produces a powerful result: women who change the world and lead the future. This isn't the post-game show; this is the second act. The best part of any show.

This is not our time to pull back, give up, or be silent. We don't have to let the youthful hard-bodied women of the world take the microphone. Good Lord, some of them don't even know about chin hairs yet. This is OUR TIME. The world needs us. Not only because of what we are doing right now, but because of what we have done. What we know, what we've lived and seen. We are the captains of this team we call womanhood, and God is not done with us.

So, instead of sitting in the shadows, let's climb up to mountaintops and stand united for the world to see us. Let's not allow ourselves to be forgotten, dismissed, or underestimated—we still have beautiful, rich contributions to offer this world. We are still here, and we are better than ever before.

Here's to the next FIDDY.

One

Did the Fat Lady Sing?

It's Not Over; It's the Second, Most Exciting Half of the Game

*T*he best is yet to come.

Is it? Is the best *really* yet to come?

When you read the intro, what did you think? Oh. You didn't read the intro, did you? I get that, I really do, because I always skip the introduction in books. If it were important, it would be in a real chapter, right? I'm a reluctant reader and just want to get to the meat of the book. But this time, don't follow my example. Actually read the intro because I spent a lot of time writing it, and, I must say, it's good, with lots of meat.

Okay, let's try again.

When you read the intro, what did you think? Did you agree? Or did it make you roll your eyes a little? There are still times I look at the evidence of my melting jowls and chest and am tempted to conclude the best is behind me. The fat lady has sung; the show is over. And you might too. Do you have that itty-bitty internal voice whispering, *Your awesome years are over, Sis, so order some Depends and call it a day?*

I'm here to tell you, your little voice is a big fat liar. Your best days are still to come, the fat lady is still belting out rich, soul-stirring anthems, and there are incredibly absorbent pads that don't show under your pants but work just as well as Depends.

Hitting our "midlife" does not mean it's time to plop down and watch the clock until we get called to join that big *Golden Girls* reunion in the sky. We're *halfway through* our lives. There's a lot of juicy stuff between the dreams of our youth and celestial coffee with Betty White.

But I'm the first to acknowledge that my life does not look anything like I thought it would. For instance, I never graced the cover of a single issue of *Seventeen* magazine, nor was I in any of the Bonne Bell lip gloss ads. I've never traveled the world on my custom pink 747 jet with cream shag carpet and ruffled curtains, and, worst of all, I did not marry Scott Baio on a cliff in Ireland. The reality that all my dreams did not come to fruition is heartbreaking.

On the flip side, I never imagined the life that God did have for me—the gifts of my children, my husbands (yes, two of them, but not at the same time), my family, my precious friends, and even my pets. I never dreamed I would get divorced, lose my sweet daughter Madison to a rare bacterial pneumonia, or that I'd battle breast cancer, lose my sister to cancer, and have an alcoholic husband. But when I look back at it all woven together, the heartaches and the joy, I see the most spectacular, vibrant fabric of a life.

(I have to pause here for a moment. I've looked back at that last paragraph several times with tears in my eyes. I don't think many people would take a glance at my past and think it was a good one. But my first half has already been one of the most beautiful and joyful lives imaginable.)

Our past is rarely what we imagined it would be in our youth. I think a lot of us at the midlife point find ourselves looking back with a sense of grief. We're grieving the person we thought we'd be and the life we thought we'd have. When we were in our early twenties, we deeply believed that everything was ahead of us and anything was possible. We weren't necessarily thinking about what those everythings were or maintaining a carefully curated list of ambitious goals; we just had a vague underlying feeling that we had endless time and boundless potential. An assumption that (if you'll forgive me overusing this phrase) the best was yet to come.

So why do we, standing at this midpoint in our lives, not continue to look ahead with the same sense of hope and expectation? Why don't we still believe that the best is yet to come? I suspect that part of the problem is, well, us. Sometime around age forty-five we start to draw this invisible line marking our past to the left and our future to the right. We believe that all the big moments and miracles are on one side, while the other side is devoid of beautiful, rich adventures and surprises. There's this lie that drifts through our minds, and it whispers, *God's greatest miracles in your life were already handed out.*

I admit that as I was approaching fifty, I had accepted some of that nonsense in my own life. I'd received so many unfathomable mercies and blessings (I mean, did I mention I crushed cancer?) that there was no possible way God had more for me. Therefore,

I wasn't deserving of a second half loaded with as much goodness as my first half.

Intellectually I know God doesn't work that way. But for a while it's how I felt, and I think it's the way a lot of us feel.

What changed it for me was a little miracle God tossed me when I was forty-seven years old. This was right about the time I decided underwire bras were for the birds and that I might be capable of growing a full goatee on my face. So, not exactly feeling my most ambitious.

However, as anybody who's read *Laughing Through the Ugly Cry* knows, I was awakened in the night by God calling me to write a book. And not just to write that book but also to leave a career that I loved and to trust in Him because He had "more for me." Now, that sounds all well and good, but have you ever walked around telling people God called you to something? I don't care how much of a believer a person is, they still think you're just a little bit cray-cray. Heck, even I thought I was a loon half the time, wondering if maybe I'd had some bad meat the night of the dream and was just super gassy. I doubted and questioned often, but I *did* move forward. Maybe not at the pace of moving to the freezer when I know there's a Cherry Garcia ice cream waiting for me, but I moved.

Everything that happened next is so ridiculous it could only come from God.

I left my career in sales at Mary Kay cosmetics and spent five months writing my first book, a process that began with a simple Google search of "How do you write a book?" (Spoiler alert—you just start writing.) Google told me the next step after writing it was to create a book proposal. That proposal was to be sent to literary agents in hopes that one would represent your book to the publishers.

My friends who were authors said that your literary agent can't be just any literary agent; you must find one who has a relationship with all the big dogs, like HarperCollins, Random House, Simon and Schuster, and so on. Oh, and you need at least twenty thousand followers on social media, and by the way, those connected literary agents are not taking queries. So good luck. And if, like Moses parting the Red Sea, you *do* get a literary agent, that agent will present your book to the publishing houses, although the chances are pretty good they'll turn it down. So again, good luck.

Very uplifting advice.

If you don't know anything about the publishing world, let me just say, it's one of the most difficult industries to break into. Your mama has to know Billy's mama and then they meet at Ms. Clara's on the third Thursday of each month (but only if there's a full moon) to decide whether they're going to take on any books about green crickets because last year they quit publishing green cricket books and only wanted books about pink and yellow crickets.

You get the picture—it's hard.

Nevertheless, I continued to move forward. I completed my book proposal and sent it to my friend Lara Casey, asking if it looked like I'd done what I was supposed to do. Within hours Lara, who is a successful, published author and entrepreneur, responded asking if she could send the book proposal to her agent, and within twenty-four hours I was signed by one of the top literary agencies out of New York. Within ninety days the amazing Claudia Cross presented the book to HarperCollins/Thomas Nelson and they signed me.

In May of 2020, my book released, and even in the pandemic landscape, it became a bestseller. I was named ECPA's New Christian Author of the Year at the ripe ol' age of fifty.

Yes, that was all God, but notice that He made it all happen—this new career, this new life—on the *right* side of that line. You know, the side where there wasn't supposed to be any monumental happenings—the boring side, the slow side, the sad side.

One of the most unexpected revelations I had during that journey was that this didn't happen despite my age; it happened *because* of my age. I began to see that as unqualified and insecure as this ol' girl felt, it was my experiences from the *past* that enabled me to thrive in this new beginning. Let me explain.

Before taking the giant leap of faith to leave my job and write my first book, I'd had my faith cemented by years and years of God carrying me through difficult times. And when I took the giant leap, I was able to call on my years of experience as one of the top ten sales directors in the nation with Mary Kay cosmetics, where I led a team of hundreds of women. For example, I regularly held meetings and events online and in person, helping to educate and inspire women, rallying them to see the value and purpose in what we were doing.

So imagine my excitement when I learned that prior to the release of *Laughing Through the Ugly Cry*, my publisher wanted to form a launch team for the book. It would involve a private Facebook group with 100 to 150 women who would support the launch of the new book, and they would hire someone to manage it. Now, I didn't know much about the publishing world, but I darn sure knew about leading groups of women, on or off Facebook. I was made for this sort of thing, and I assured my publishing team there was no need to hire outside help.

We ended up with an incredible army of over five hundred women. But that didn't happen by magic. It was the skill and wisdom and faith gained in my past that equipped me to gather and harness the power of these beautiful blessings. Never in a million years would I have imagined that the things I learned from Mary Kay cosmetics would serve me well in launching a book that I (*me!*) had written. And thankfully, as we will talk about later, I didn't have to do it alone. Working with those women was an immense blessing and confidence builder, and they were integral to the successful launch of my book.

But that's life, isn't it? When we step into anything new, our confidence is down. We can, however, build our confidence through the repetition of doing something. Like, the more you make a grilled cheese sandwich, the better you get at it, and your confidence increases. (I just so happen to make a mean grilled cheese sandwich—just the right amount of butter and two dreamy types of cheese grilled to perfection. I'm not a kitchen person, but my confidence is very high in the grilled cheese department.) Pivoting into this new season of life is a little bit like this. Imagine all your confidence has been formed by making grilled cheese sandwiches with cheddar on basic white bread, using equipment you're accustomed to, and now you find yourself in a different kitchen, with different pans, and all you can find is fancy French cheeses and focaccia. And apparently you're also supposed to add a gourmet soup on the side. It's all stuff you're familiar with and yet it's all a bit different. (And yes, I'll wait while you go make a grilled cheese sandwich before you read on.)

Of course there will be learning involved. Grabbing this new season by the horns can be hard because most of us have been doing a certain something a certain way for so long, and now that something is changing. Maybe it's motherhood turning into an empty-nesthood, or life with a partner making an unexpected turn, or the sheer betrayal of our bodies giving way to age.

No matter the cause, it's a big stinkin' deal and we feel it deeply. Suddenly we feel we're part of a world that is full of round holes and we are the squarest peg of all.

I get it. I've felt invisible and irrelevant, believing I no longer had anything to offer. I really do get it.

Even with my experience of leaving Mary Kay and landing in an amazing writing career, I've dealt with continuous doubt and regret and fear—all of which I will talk about later.

But for now I'm here to tell you, friend, that just because life changes doesn't mean you aren't fully equipped for what it's about to dish out. As my own journey of becoming an author was underway, I repeatedly saw new ways in which the experiences of my past made me good at the experiences of my present. So many times I believed I was ill-equipped, too old, too irrelevant— especially when I started something new, like trying to learn the ins and outs of social media or business email lists or those stupid Instagram reels. But every time I pressed through and made myself just give it a try, I realized I have what so many of those young whippersnappers don't: wisdom and experience. Maybe I hadn't figured out how to use crazy filters in my stories, but I did know how to connect with women, even on social media. Plus, because I was in my fifties instead of my twenties, I wasn't paralyzed by the thought that everyone was laughing behind my back and whispering about my failures. I knew what worked for *me* and who I was, and I was confident enough to say no when it wasn't right for me. (I mean, I am just not going to dance and point aimlessly on a video. It's just not who I am, and that's not a bad thing.)

I was not a qualified writer. Heck, I didn't even make grocery lists. God put me at the start of a brand-new road; all I had to do was walk. I had no idea what I was doing, but the more I walked, the more it became clear to me that my past had made the new journey possible.

And you don't have to be a pink-Cadillac-driving, makeup-pushing Southerner to discover that you are indeed prepared for whatever this second half brings. I can pull just as much wisdom from the brief stint in my early thirties of selling gourmet pickles (yes, I really did that) as I can from my many years of organizing Mary Kay meetings. Or let's go even further back. Before I immersed myself in the pickle market, I spent ten years in media sales and marketing. How's that for a pivot? Having to go from selling ad space to understanding the intricacies of the brining process taught me I could learn something new quickly and—after a few short months—I could be *good* at it. Those pickles were why I believed I could step into the publishing world, which I knew nothing about, and trust that with time I could learn and succeed.

It turns out my former failures and successes created a beautiful launching pad for the adventures of my future. It's been far from being the beginning of the end that I believed it would be.

It must grieve God to watch us sacrifice our future promises on the altars of our fears. God is NOT done with us. We have so much more to offer, more to say, and more to give than in any other season of life. Our fears and insecurities are no surprise to Him, and He will use every piece of us if we let Him: the good, the bad, and the ugly. This season of life is not the end of anything unless we let it be. It's most definitely not the time to slam both feet onto the brakes and screech to a standstill. This time is an awakening, a jolt, a recalibration enabling us to refocus and do the things we are more equipped than ever to do.

The world needs you now. Not you when you finally get in shape, or finish that course, or clean out that kitchen drawer, or learn to do whatever. If you pull back now and stop taking chances and living full out, your story will fizzle out unnecessarily. And that would be the saddest story of all. But you can make the decision right now that this is only the *middle* of the story, and your story is getting better and better. Its pages will be filled with tales of twists and turns and love and adventure. Because you, my sweet friend, have more to give now than ever before. Don't turn in a book at the end of Part 1; the second half is always the best half. (Except my books, which are equally best in both halves.)

I'm not saying that this season is easy. It's not. It's strange and filled with questioning and doubt. But inside, past the melting body parts and the reading glasses, we have learned more, loved more, and even lost more than we ever thought possible when we were in our early twenties.

So get ready, because the only fat (okay, slightly overweight) lady singing around here is me—with an out-of-tune version of Helen Reddy's "I Am Woman, Hear Me Roar." I'm all in for the mighty second half, and I hope you'll sing with me as we step into the best years of our lives!

two

The Shift

Accept Your Personal Fight with Aging

When I began writing a book encouraging women to be their best selves in the middle of their life and beyond, one unavoidable truth seemed to be circling me at every turn: I might have to admit to myself that I was right there with them. Actually, I needed to do more than just admit it. I needed to fully embrace that sucker like a good pair of Spanx on a fifty-year-old butt. But for some absurd reason, I just couldn't wrap my head around being this age.

In early 2022 I began hosting retreats for women in my home. When I launched the retreats on social media, they sold out quickly, and then I sent my attendees a questionnaire about everything from their age to what they hoped to get out of their retreat time. I reviewed their answers and then called my husband, Craig, into the room.

"I'm a little surprised at the age of the women who are attending these retreats," I told him. "They're almost all in their fifties and sixties."

He paused, looked at me, and said, "Well yeah, they're all your age."

His words felt like the knockout punch from Mike Tyson's right hook. Those women were all my age? That was ridiculous. I mean I was only . . . yep, fifty-two.

Why was I genuinely surprised? How could it be that despite my author head being fully immersed every day in stories of women living their best lives after fifty, and despite the fact that I was thriving personally, my visceral reaction was that I didn't belong in this demographic? Clearly, my subconscious perception of what a woman in her fifties, sixties, and seventies is like differed from the reality I was observing and experiencing. If I am being completely honest, I believed that being in one's "midlife" was a bad thing. A *really* bad thing.

Despite all evidence to the contrary, in my confused mind, hitting my fifties and beyond meant sailing away into the land of the forgotten, used, and has-been. I was not that person! I was still working on books and speaking and hoping to maybe change the world a little.

I worried that if I really was that woman in her fifties, people would think I was out of touch, or that I no longer understood the ways of the world because I didn't have a TikTok account (honestly, I really don't get it). Or maybe people would only see my swinging turkey neck and flabby arms and believe that I'm just too old to be a part of the conversation anymore. I was terrified of becoming irrelevant to the world.

There was some serious cognitive dissonance going on. Every

day my heart and soul were bursting with joy as I wrote chapters of this book and planned my retreat about embracing the second half, and yet I'd entered into my late forties and fifties with as much grace and acceptance as a bank robber in a bad cop movie. Father Time was the man in blue chasing me, and I was the hardened criminal running for my life down alleys and over fences, doing anything to elude the cuffs of aging. In my mind, the grass certainly did not look greener in that second half of life. In fact, it looked a lot like dying grass in the midst of a hot Southern summer. Nothing about getting older was inviting to me.

And yet, I knew many thriving and happy women in their fifties and beyond. So why, if the second-half crowd was so dynamic and accomplished and spectacular, wasn't I thrilled to be part of it?

I know that an ungrateful transition into my fifties like I experienced is not uncommon among women, and I'd like to think it's not my fault (things rarely are—ask my husband). I've been brainwashed to think this way, right? I blame social media, Hollywood, and all those magazines at the grocery store checkout. I blame the mannequins in the windows and the Peloton Instagram ads. The story is always the same: look younger, dress younger, eat younger, just BE younger. The message is clear: old bad, young good. Thanks for coming. Good night.

It doesn't help when those around us inadvertently reinforce the message. Several years ago at a Mary Kay conference, my dear friend Wendy shared with me that her feelings were hurt because some of our younger colleagues had been asking her to *take* the photos rather than be in them. I'm sure I said something reassuring, but I didn't give it much thought. Then, a few years later, I was at a Mary Kay event without her and *I* got asked several times to take a photo of the younger girls. Wait, what? I was devastated and it hurt my feelings too. Wendy and I had gone from being *in* the pictures to taking them. When did that happen?

But, back to the retreat . . . my conversation with Craig about the women coming to my retreat compelled me to ask myself: *What if I can't blame the world for this one? What if I'm part of the problem? What if I'm choosing to believe a story that's all wrong, and choosing to accept the photographer role instead of pushing my way back into the photo?* The idea of me being part of the problem was in and of itself a miracle moment because, again, as my husband will tell you, I'm rarely to blame (*she types and giggles*). Did I need to rewrite the story I'd been repeating in my mind for decades?

Maybe. Let's look at the evidence.

I've been looking at past Dawns longingly for as many years as I can remember. Right now I look at forty-year-old me and see how much firmer my legs were. When I was forty, I looked at thirty-year-old me and saw what seemed like a perfect body devoid of cancer scars and mastectomies. Younger, to me, was always better.

It's not just about having a firmer body with two matching breasts that don't hang out from under my arms. My most emotionally devastating birthday was at the ripe ol' age of twenty-eight. I was divorced, living in Austin, Texas, and was a single mom to Makenzie. I was going through a deep depression over being so far off the mark of where I thought I would be at that age with my career and a partner. I remember the feelings of debilitating sadness, of thinking the world was done with me and that I was too old to do anything more. It's easy to be twenty years out and laugh a little at that. But I felt those feelings deeply, and you know what? It's not unlike how I felt at thirty-six, forty-one, and fifty.

I have been telling myself so many ridiculous untruths for so long. No matter my age, I've always looked back at a younger version of myself and thought, *Wow, I really had it going on. Why didn't I celebrate that?* It's easy to miss it as it's happening, but the pattern is there. In my fifties, I had to recognize this: if I am still looking at pictures from my late thirties and thinking *Wow, she was amazing,* then it is reasonable to suspect that at seventy I will think the same about the woman I am today, and then at eighty about who I was at seventy, and so on—unless I changed something.

It was time, I realized, for a full rewrite.

In my attempts to edit the untruths of aging, I've begun to notice that a huge part of what we focus on as the years go by is the physical—our bodies, our wrinkles, our aches and pains. Granted, none of us like the physical aspects of aging, right? Well, except maybe when we were twelve and hoping for boobs—but other than that, we do not want any of the things Father Time is delivering to us physically.

Yes, those changes are a big part of who we are but certainly not the only part. In fact, I would argue that physical signs of aging are only a small part of all the marvelous things that encompass this beautiful season.

We think we want the figure of our twenties, with warp-speed metabolism, rich hair colors devoid of grays, and firm, tight skin that doesn't ripple like a bowl of Jell-O, but I don't know a single woman who would want the brain of that same hard-bodied beauty. You couldn't pay me enough money to go back to that young woman, firm butt and all. I wouldn't want any part of the woman I was mentally, emotionally, or spiritually. Frankly, I was an idiot. I was hot-headed, I made bad decisions continually, I judged others quickly, and I was arrogant, egotistical, and devoid of a faith in God.

But in the decades since then, my heart has softened. I've experienced great heartaches and tragedies that allow me to empathize with others and be slow to judge. I failed often and learned to get back up quickly, and this humbled my arrogant, self-centered heart. I lost ones I loved, which taught me to hold on tighter to the ones I have. Through all of it I learned that I never will be anything without the love of Jesus. It takes time to experience the things that shape us, which is why, generally, we were all idiots in our twenties. (If you are in your twenties and reading this, I am not talking to you, honey. You are perfect.)

It takes time to unravel all the glorious gifts God has in store for us. Heck, I didn't write my first book until I was fifty. I didn't know I had a gift and love for public speaking until I was forty, and I didn't have my third child until I was thirty-seven—and Ellason Rayne is one of the sweetest gifts of my life. You don't get all the gifts God has for you in your youth. You get them over time. The work is the journey of life; the reward is the gifts God gives you along the way.

Making those journeys around the sun is a beautiful and wondrous gift, if we choose to accept it. The victory is in *living* a full life each and every year. Living your life all out and being fully you, no matter the age. You in all your wondrous, quirky, beautiful glory. After all, God made only one of you. Why on earth wouldn't you celebrate that?

Here's what I have figured out: If we can't embrace who we are right now, we are missing the best part. You are the best you've ever been (I said you, not your boobs). You're overflowing with wisdom and knowledge and experiences that will enable you to help others more profoundly than ever before. Or lead a team with more love and experience. Or start a company because you understand more of the world and how it works and how people work. You're less afraid because, heck, at this point you know how to fall, and get back up, and know it's okay. You know that no matter what happens, the sun will rise and it will set. That God was, is, and forever will be on the throne, and you know this because you've aged.

As long as we keep believing a Hollywood story that tells us with each year we become less, then we are a part of the problem. The thought that a woman in her forties, fifties, sixties, and beyond is any less than the woman she was the year before is a big ol' stinky lie. And the longer we stay silent about it, the more women there will be out there believing it.

Wait. Did I say I figured it out? What I mean is, I figured it out *for now*.

The patterns of my past have taught me that there is no line in the sand, and it isn't just a moment of acceptance about our season or age. We don't have one light-bulb moment when complete contentment washes over our bodies and we are set for life. Whatever acceptance I'm feeling today might be replaced a few years from now by sixty-year-old Dawn looking back wistfully at some aspect of my life today and wanting to scream at present-day me for taking it for granted.

And that's okay. These moments might feel like sorrowful endings for a little while, but they can become sweet awakenings. Gifts. These are pivot points in life, seasons of reevaluation, which can lead to a time of rebirth. We get to look at where we are, grieve a little about what we aren't, or maybe even grieve where we have been. Perhaps let go of what we thought life would be or who we would be, and celebrate that God is making us new every day. In the next chapter of your story, He is going to reveal His greatest miracles in your life, and I am here to tell you it will not look how you thought it would.

I've finally accepted that I am in my fifties and have embraced that it's a fantastically awesome place to be. The shackles of lies are off; I will not look at my younger days with longing, and I will not wait five years only to look back at today with regret. I am fully here. And if any of that starts to change, I'm coming back to reread this chapter.

three

Hello You

Define the New You and Find Your Passion

I have a ridiculously *huge* closet. I'm talking 610 square feet, which is about the same size as my first apartment. It's the kind of closet women pray to Jesus to deliver to them, a divine closet of movie stars, fairy tales, and little ol' me. It has twenty-four large drawers, over thirty feet of bar hanging space, and over seventy-four feet of shelving JUST FOR SHOES. And that's only my side.

When we first moved into this house, our daughter Ellason *lived* in that closet for a couple of years while we built an addition to our home. Our system made sense because at the time we only had two bedrooms (don't ask me who designs a house with a six-hundred-foot closet but only two bedrooms), and my mother-in-law was in the other bedroom. But yeah, it didn't sound great when Ella went to school and told her new friends that she slept in her parents' closet every night.

You get my point—I have a massive closet.

But guess what? The size is not why I love it. To understand why I now take great joy in standing inside my weirdly big closet, you need to first know what happened in my previous not-so-big closet.

When I was living in my last house, which had a more normal bedroom-to-closet size ratio, I decided one day to spend the afternoon organizing my clothes. Here's how I like things arranged: shirts with no sleeves graduating into short sleeves, then long sleeves, and each of those shirt categories arranged from dark to light in color. There's a similar system with dresses and pants; I do the entire closet by length and color. Trust me, it's the only way that really makes sense.

So, you know how when you're in the midst of a big cleaning or organizational session, you can't really see the final product? You're in the zone, focused on the minutiae, like trying to decide whether to keep that wad of tights that are too shredded to go with skirts but could serve in a pinch under a pair of palazzo pants. It's not until you leave and return that you have the objectivity to fully enjoy the fruits of your labor.

Well, that's what happened to me. With fresh eyes the next morning, I could see that, while my closet was organized, it held a wardrobe of sadness. It looked like a garment trailer for the most depressing movie ever made; it was a *Sophie's Choice* of black, gray, and beige sweaters and leggings. Most of it was dark, dark, dark, dripping in melancholy. A singular thought shot through my mind over and over: *When did I quit wearing colors?*

I used to love to wear colors. They made me happy and gave

me little bursts of confidence, a polychromatic vivacious fierceness I could feel. Corals, pinks, oranges, and reds made up my personal palette. But somehow, bit by bit, I'd unconsciously transitioned to dark clothes.

After some reflection, I had to admit it wasn't because I was striving for some Morticia Addams vibe or because I'd seen *The Matrix* one too many times. The real reason behind that transition was that I had become a woman who dressed to look thinner and less conspicuous to the outside world. For me, these clothes, devoid of all color and happiness, were a cloak for my insecurity; they were a visual representation of how I'd been feeling for a long time. Feeling thin had become more important than feeling joyful. Now let's be clear: does looking skinny make me feel happy? Heck yes! But enjoying clothing is about so much more than feeling thin, and in that moment, I realized I'd lost a big part of who I was.

The very next day I had another epiphany, this time at the grocery store. (This was before I decided to boycott in-person grocery shopping forever and sold my soul to Instacart.) I sported my usual grocery-going attire—black yoga pants that had never been to yoga, no makeup, and some sort of half attempt at a ponytail. This was my uniform. I did my usual perusing of the aisles and then, just when I was trying to decide between diced or chunky canned tomatoes, everything stopped. Piping through the sound system of the store was Luciano Pavarotti singing "Nessun Dorma," one of my favorite operatic songs.

Yes, I'm talking about opera. I know that's throwing you a little, but I'm super cultured and all. This song provoked so much emotion from me that my body physically reacted; goosebumps literally appeared up and down my arms, and my perpetually tensed shoulders dropped down from my ears. Pavarotti's voice billowing through the speakers was hypnotizing. For the second day in a row, I found myself asking a difficult question. This time it was, *When did I quit listening to music that stirred my soul?*

Maybe the initial answer to that one isn't such a mystery; I suspect I quit listening to soul-stirring music somewhere between Dora the Explorer and Hannah Montana, when my musical choices became those of my child. But she had since moved on and discovered her own albums and playlists of music that touched her. Why hadn't I?

These two small but profound moments in my life occurred within forty-eight hours of each other and quickly became the catalyst for a journey of discovery. A determined journey to fall back in love with myself.

Because if we are going to live the next half of our lives better than the first, we have to get back in touch with who we are and what makes us happy.

For me, this meant getting back to the mindset of the twenty-something me who loved herself and saw the years ahead as bursting with life to live. The girl who could stay up dancing till 2 a.m. and still make it to work on time because she was racing to be the top producer and establish a name for herself. That girl also believed she could eat salad for a day and drop six pounds (I mean, I'm pretty sure I could). I needed to re-become that woman ready to explode at the possibilities of my future.

I don't know how we go from that kind of passion-filled salad woman capable of anything to the chronically fatigued lady in an almost-ponytail and yogaless yoga pants. There aren't warning signs or flashing-light moments in life that shout, "Hey, watch out sister, you left some of your sparkle back at Tammy Jo's house when her husband asked if you were pregnant three years after your last baby." I wish we could see where we dropped little pieces of ourselves so we'd know where to pick them back up. But we can't. Instead, we have to dust off those yoga pants and start something new. To acknowledge that there is so much more in us than what we are *feeling*. Because there absolutely is.

My little search party for myself was almost like a boy courting a girl. Not by sending myself a "u up?" text at midnight but in the unrealistic movie way where he is so infatuated with her that he goes to the ends of the earth to learn all her likes and dislikes. I wanted to remember everything that made me happy, and I wanted to be on purpose about it. I was going to fall back in love with the woman in the mirror.

It took several weeks of analyzing my thoughts and behaviors. I paid close attention to the little things and the big things. I wrote down songs I had forgotten ever existed, and I walked around like a glue-sniffing addict smelling everything from my perfumes and lotions to candles and fabric softeners. I sat and thought about the colors that had stopped filling my closet; I observed the pillows and accent pieces in my house, asking myself, *How does this make me FEEL?*

And then I did the hardest thing of all. I stood naked in front of a mirror and made myself really look at what was in front of me. Have you ever done this? IT'S HARD. I started at the top and worked my way down, thanking my body for all that it was. I thanked God for giving me "good hair" and for it coming back after cancer. I thanked Him for my eyes that could see and for the ability to smell all my favorite things. I even thanked Him for my turkey neck, albeit through clenched teeth. *A turkey neck*, I thought to myself, *is better than no neck at all.*

I stared at my breasts, these cut-up, reshaped, formerly cancer-ridden mounds on my body. One with a nipple and one built from the skin and muscles on my tummy, leaving me a scar from hip to hip. I was angry, and I was grateful. This body was covered in evidence of one of the most difficult seasons in my life—and one of the most beautiful seasons. Even as I thanked God, I cried.

But I also giggled. I touched the baby-making stretch marks, silvery lines that once mortified me and now just make me smile because they remind me of my children's births. My body had become a wild treasure map of stories and a crazy, beautiful life well lived. That day, by the time I reached my toes, I loved every inch of myself. In that moment, I knew my body was beautiful.

(Did that gratitude last? Did I take to strolling languidly around the house in my birthday suit every morning, feeling proud and content? Gosh, no. Loving my body is a challenge I have to face time and time again. But I learned that day it is possible and it is powerful.)

I began showing appreciation for myself in other ways too, like, just *trying* harder. I started taking real showers again, the kind that involve loofahs and shaving my legs and putting lotion on afterward. (I'd pretty much given up shaving my legs when I realized Craig would joyfully take me hairy or smooth.) I chose clothes that had no elastic bands; I put makeup on, and blow-dried and curled my hair. I danced, really danced, in front of a mirror, in my room, and down the hall . . . I just danced. (How long has it been since you really danced?) I sang out loud because I LOVE to sing. No one else likes when I sing, but I do.

It was as if I had forgotten that all of these were once parts of myself that I loved, and finally I was remembering.

These small things made me want to pay attention to the

bigger things. I already knew I did *not* like to cook or clean, but what else could I say about myself with certainty? I examined more of my behaviors, my habits, my preferences. For instance, contrary to what I tried to believe for much of my adult life, I fully embraced that I'm a morning person. I like to go to bed at 8:30 p.m.; I like to wake up around 5 a.m. I don't particularly like a schedule; I'm more of an "I'll get it done sometime between 6 a.m. and 11 a.m." kind of girl. I'm not a person who thrives on packed days and layered deadlines, because I like some wiggle room for fun and family. (This one is hard to admit in a culture that glorifies staying busy.) And you know something else? I realized I would rather work eighty hours a week for myself than work forty hours for anyone else because I'm a die-hard entrepreneur. Recognizing all this made me happy.

It was an eye-opening journey of self-discovery. For the first time in years, I felt like I knew who I was, and I liked it. I wrote every revelation down and later added that list to the notes section on my phone. This way I can remind myself of all that I love and can easily add to it when new loves appear or I hear a new song that makes me happy.

I was becoming a better version of myself because I was reminded of what DAWN BARTON loved. I defined who I was, and best of all, I accepted what I was not. I was discovering the best, most beautiful version of myself.

Now listen, is all that—the shaved legs, the kitchen shimmy, the coral wraparound dress—the answer to redefining the second half? Do we rediscover the things we once loved and declare it all a success? Of course not. We're only on chapter 3 here.

But this is an essential first step. Remember that twenty-something we talked about a while ago? The girl who was full of confidence and optimism about the years ahead, and had a wardrobe she was proud of and a jam-packed CD tower of music she loved? We need to get back into that headspace, where we take care of ourselves and prioritize ourselves and believe our goals matter.

If you're like me, you've spent the last few decades bending and giving and morphing to serve so many different people and jobs and communities that you're no longer sure what's left of you. You find yourself looking right and left, searching for some semblance of the woman you once were. You don't know which way to go, because you don't know what you want. That's okay, neither did I.

It is natural to have seasons in life when you feel a little lost, like you've forgotten who you are. What isn't natural is to *stay* in that. This is not the time to be fixated on what you didn't become or didn't do. That's done. No one will ever fight harder for you or know what you need more than YOU. Only *you* can figure out how to fall back in love with you.

When you love you, you think about you. You rediscover your interests, you set your own goals for the future and define the woman you hope to be, even if you're still figuring out who that woman is as you go along. I once heard someone say, "A moving target is hard to hit, but an invisible one is impossible." Goals for what we want and who we want to be can change or evolve, but if we never define what those goals are, how on earth will we know what to strive for? Whoa.

For the record, in all this I'm using the word *goal* loosely. The definition of a beautiful second half is different for all of us. Perhaps for you, the second half is about slowing down, retiring, and relaxing; for someone else it might be about chasing dreams of travel or launching a business idea that's been tucked away for years.

Either way, the not-so-secret secret to happiness and fulfillment is pursuing what matters to you. It doesn't have to be about *one* passion in life. It's about pursuing all the things that appeal to you. Heck, if there's one thing we learned in the last thirty years of adulting, it's that pursuing a single goal relentlessly is a real recipe for disappointment, right?

But it's hard to set goals when we don't believe we can achieve them. It's hard to think about setting goals when we haven't set aside time to buy a new bra in eight years. That's why the first step is falling back in love with yourself. I've included an "I Love Me" Challenge on page 29 to help you get started and to get you back in the headspace of paying attention to YOU.

If you're going to lead the charge into a fulfilling and beautiful second half of your life, make sure the leader of that charge is someone you love. Going into our second half with a fraction of our best selves doesn't serve the world. It doesn't honor God or our yoga pants. We have to put ourselves at the center again and pull ourselves out from under whatever layers life has buried us under—raising kids, work, cleaning dog poop off the dining room floor again because no one took the dog out. This is your time of rediscovery. And without this, I'm sorry to tell you, the rest of it will not work.

After my journey of discovery, I know I am the most perfectly and uniquely qualified person on the planet to pursue the dreams and goals of *my* next half. I'm open to discovering my next passion. I have a new self-love and confidence and am ready to learn new things with the eagerness I had in my twenties. Well, unless we're talking about a new exercise class. I'm not really eager for that.

I want you to make your own discoveries. I want you to interrogate your deepest self and pull all that makes you *you* back to the surface. Your process might not be the same as mine, but even figuring out where to begin and what questions to ask can be part of the journey.

And if you're feeling a little stuck or intimidated by the whole idea, I have good news. The next chapter is a veritable treasure trove of tips for falling back in love with yourself.

Four

The "I Love Me" Challenge

Twenty-One Days Back to Loving You

*I*f you follow me on social media, some of this chapter might look familiar because this is based on a challenge I issue every year, starting on Valentine's Day. I call it the "I Love Me" Challenge: fourteen days to falling back in love with YOU.

Online, I post one question per day for two weeks. People can read it and do the challenge for the day. In this book, it's a little different. I don't expect you to read one paragraph at a time and put the book away until tomorrow. Nobody wants a chapter that takes half a month to finish. Instead, I want you to read the prompts I'm going to share and begin thinking about them as you move throughout your day-to-day life. Start your data collecting; write down ideas and observations as you come back to these questions over and over.

These questions may seem simple. You may even find yourself wondering, *How on earth can these simple things bring me back to loving myself?* Trust me, when you start really looking at the little things and remembering what stirs your soul, you'll find it's like someone turned a light on inside of you.

In this book I am expanding the original online two-week challenge and making it twenty-one days: a full three weeks of falling back in love with you. I've also created a free tracking sheet you can download and print from dawnbarton.com/iloveme to help with your exploration. You'll find each of these prompts and space to record what you're discovering about yourself.

Stay firm in loving yourself and actively working to cultivate that love day after day, week after week. Anytime you're feeling up for the challenge, flip back to this chapter, choose a specific Love Me task, and dive in.

1. **What Colors Make You Happy and Bring You Joy?**

As you may know, I love corals, pinks, yellows, and oranges in my wardrobe, but my home is a different story. I like my home to be calming and soothing with white and tan colors throughout. What are your favorite colors? Look around your home, your closet, your office, your car. Where can you bring those colors into your life? Maybe it's as simple as adding your favorite flower or a light linen scarf that gives you a little skip in your step. Whatever it is for you, just start adding it in.

2. **What Music Stirs Your Soul and Makes You Feel Alive When You Hear It?**

What are the songs you once loved but no longer listen to? You know the ones. Just the sound of their very first note can send you in the direction of an entirely different mindset. What songs move you and give you all the feels? Write them down. Create musical playlists you can turn on at any time—maybe one for dancing, one for relaxing, one with music you like to listen to while cooking or cleaning or . . . doing something romantic. Stir your soul!

3. **What Fragrance Makes You Want to Stop, Close Your Eyes, and Take It In?**

Did you know that olfactory memories (smell memories) last the longest in our minds? In other words, we could forget a person's name from twenty years ago, but we could still recognize the smell of their home. Such is the power of the scents we surround ourselves with. And yet, it's easy to go years where we settle for nothing more interesting than our Spring Breeze laundry detergent and lemon kitchen counter spray.

Candles, essential oils, perfume, fresh flowers—the options are plenty. Find your smells and put them back into your life.

4. **Where Is Your Favorite Spot?**

A chair in a room upstairs or a rocker on a porch? Maybe it's not at your home but rather a bench in a park, a back-corner booth at a coffee shop, or a grassy spot under a favorite tree. Where is YOUR spot, a place that—even if only for twenty minutes—is only yours where you can go to read, to pray, or to just be fully yourself and quiet? A place that is yours and yours alone? Go there more.

5. **What Songs Make You Get Up and Dance?**

I know you're thinking we just did music, but that was more about putting the soundtrack back into your life. This is a different category of music, because there's a difference between hearing Pavarotti's "Nessun Dorma" in the canned-food aisle of Publix and feeling your body release tension and hearing the Gipsy Kings' "Bamboleo" at a sidewalk cafe and feeling compelled to start a little salsa dance with a stranger.

You gotta know your power anthems, your pick-me-ups, your go-to songs for when you need to get up and move your booty.

6. **What Is Your Favorite Feature on Your Face?**

Loving yourself is about loving the things that stir your soul, but it is also about loving the way you look and loving your body. I know for so many women, staring into a mirror and being grateful is hard. We instinctively see all the things that are wrong or we want to fix. Rarely do we just sit, look, and say to ourselves, "I have alert, honest eyes" or "My skin is soft and it's filled with small lines that remind me I have laughed often" or "My smile is beautiful and real and joyful." Look at yourself in the mirror and notice all there is to love. You are God's masterpiece whether or not you believe it, and He wants you to appreciate His beautiful, unique creation.

7. **What Is Your Favorite Feature on Your Body?**

Is your body perfect? No. And that's okay. Steer clear of negative self-talk by starting from a place of gratitude for a body that is *here*, is healthy, and works (even if it only *mostly* works). Every day I have the choice to view my body as a hot mess—or as a glorious reminder that *I am here*. If I look at it with eyes of love, I can always find plenty to cherish. So just stop and choose one thing. One feature that you can point to and say, "I really do like that." While you're at it, find another one.

8. **Stand in Front of a Mirror Without Clothes on and Thank God.**

Now that you've rediscovered a couple of features of your face and body to cherish, it's time to pause and admire the whole wonderful darn thing. Starting with the hair on your head, all the way down to your toes, thank God for it. I know, you may be dropping your jaw or wincing, but trust me on this one. It's a miraculous exercise. Truly look at every single part of your body and THANK GOD. Yes, even your thighs and upper arms. THANK HIM! This is an emotional challenge, but please know it will be freeing. Do it often.

9. **What Books Take You Away?**

What books do you love? Don't waste time on books you feel you *should* read. What books do you *want* to read? If you haven't read for a while, ask your friends what they're reading, or think about what you were drawn to back when you read more often. Whether you prefer audiobooks, Kindles, shiny new hardcovers, or old-fashioned paperbacks you can take in the bath, dive into something that interests YOU.

Next, get a book! And read it.

10. **What Is Your Best Time of Day?**

When is your sweet spot? Are you a night owl? A

morning girl? When is your most powerful time of the day, when you are the best you? Be intentional about how you use this time. Try to plan your most important tasks and activities in this space. What in your day deserves the best of you?

My best time is early—really early. That's when my mind is clear and I do well with creative and strategic thinking. Once 3 p.m. hits, forming complete sentences is nearly impossible. Because of this I've learned to schedule anything important early in my day. What about you?

11. **Who Needs to Hear That You're Thinking About Them?**

You know those times when you randomly think of someone you haven't talked to in a while—maybe a name or face comes to mind, or a memory? Those are little nudges and whispers to do a little something to connect. The next time you have one of those moments, take just a few minutes to reach out. No one ever regretted telling another person that they love them, care about them, and are grateful for them. And while this is a beautiful way to bless somebody else, you'll be pleasantly surprised by what a lift your soul will get out of this interaction.

12. **How Can You Up Your Hair and Makeup Regimen Today?**

Maybe this won't become a new daily routine, but there's something fun and exciting about sitting down and taking the time to really style our hair and put on ALL of our makeup. The kind we only reserve for special events. Maybe it sounds silly that some good mascara and a curling iron could help transform our insides, but they can and they do. I worked in cosmetics for ten years and watched women cry after they put on makeup because they'd forgotten how amazing they could look.

Now, before you get all worked up about me subscribing to superficial standards, let's be clear: YES, YOU ARE ENOUGH WITHOUT MAKEUP. If you don't like it, don't wear it. You do you! I just want you to be aware that focusing extra on your appearance—even doing something little—can really change your mindset and emotional state and remind you of how much YOU love YOU. Remember, God thinks you are exquisite no matter what. I just want you to remember it too!

13. **What Would an Ideal Day Look Like to You?**

No appointments, no to-dos—what would this day look like for you? The trick here is to keep it ambitious yet realistic. No jets to Paris or foot massages by Jon Hamm. For me, the ideal day starts before the sunrise because seeing the sun come up gives me the most ridiculous amount of joy. Then coffee on my porch, worship music streaming from Alexa on the side table as I spend a little time with Jesus in prayer or reading. Afterward, I'd grab Craig's hand and we'd take our morning walk with the dogs at a slow pace, taking in all that nature offers up to us. A little computer work, lunch at George's Bistro with Craig, a little more work (yes, I actually enjoy working), and then dinner with the family. In a perfect world, I would be fast asleep by nine.

Now, plan what *your* perfect day looks like from the moment you wake up. Put that in your calendar—you deserve at least one ideal day a year. If possible, put it in there several more times. Then book the appointments, make the reservations, tell your bestie to save the date. Take the steps now to ensure it happens.

14. When Was the Last Time You Purchased New Undergarments?

Undergarments, you say? Yep. Your panties, your bras, your delicates . . . whatever you want to call them. When was the last time you bought new, pretty ones for yourself? Let's toss those old ugly things out and get knickers that make us feel good about ourselves! Call me progressive, but I don't think we're supposed to wear the same ones for seventeen years.

Annnd it doesn't have to be something all lacy. I have a girlfriend who bought me Wonder Woman panties when I was going through cancer treatment, and I still love wearing them, especially for special occasions. Heck, guess what I had on underneath that dignified black suit I wore when I gave my first TED Talk?

You deserve to feel pretty and special. Girl, go get a new bra!

15. What Is Your Favorite Way to Move Your Body?

Let's be clear, I'd rather be eating some spicy jambalaya than getting up and moving my body. I'm not a person who has learned to enjoy this thing called exercise. Nope, not even a little. But here's what I know: getting your blood flowing doesn't have to be miserable or come with a membership at a gym. It can be relaxing and enjoyable when you focus not on calories or sweat but on feeling good and clearing your head. I love to walk around the perimeter of our property, watching the dogs, leaving my phone behind and just breathing. I also love to swim. What's your thing? How can you weave more of it into your day-to-day life?

Don't know what your thing is? Go on a mission to find it. Ask friends what they do; check the community center for activities or opportunities you might not have known existed. Sign up for a sport you haven't played in decades, or jump into the newest craze. Did you know pickleball is a thing? And ax throwing? Certainly there's something equally unexpected and fun in your town.

16. **What's Your Go-To Outfit for Feeling Super Mega-Fabulous?**

I want you to find your one superhero outfit. You know, that outfit that makes you feel like you can take on the day and make all things happen? That one. What is hanging in that closet of yours that you love? Quit saving it and start wearing it more. This is not a dress rehearsal.

17. **Who Fills Your Cup?**

This one thing I know for sure: who you spend your time with matters. Your family, your friends, your coworkers, it all matters. Respecting and loving ourselves means that we spend time with people who lift us up, fill our cups, and treat us well. We walk away feeling good after we've been with them, not worse.

Make a list of these people and make a plan for spending more time with them. You are far too magnificent of a woman to be anything but loved and lifted, my sweet friend.

18. **What Is Your Favorite Meal?**

Seems simple, doesn't it? Eat your favorite food. But it's possible that you have served and loved others so well for so long that you have forgotten what it is that *you* love. For me, it's Nanny's shrimp-and-okra gumbo or Mawmaw's decadent cinnamon chocolate cake. But I also love a huge salad with chicken, lime rice, black beans, and lime dressing. (I know, it's not very "salady" but it does have lettuce, so it counts.) Remind yourself of what you love to eat, write it down, and then—you guessed it—go enjoy it!

19. **Where Would You Like to Take a Trip To?**

Putting aside practicalities like budget and free time, where do *you* want to go? Not with the family or girl-friends, just a place you want to experience? During what season of the year? For how long? What sort of activities do you want to do when you get there? After you really define it, then you can add in the people (or not!), but first it just has to be a place YOU want to go.

For this one, I'm not going to say, "Okay, now go book it!" (I mean, if you can, then do.) That's not actually the purpose of this exercise. This is about getting back in touch with your passions, your dreams, your priorities. You might find it's harder than expected to draw up a perfect plan, since your past trips and travels were probably designed around everything but YOU.

20. **Do You Know What Makes You Feel Loved?**

This is not as easy as you might think because we are all different. This is the point where I highly recommend you read *The Five Love Languages* by Gary Chapman—or, at a minimum, go to his website and take the online quiz. Understanding how you feel loved makes life ever so much easier; it equips you to better communicate your needs to your partner and loved ones, and it helps you be more for-giving of others when they disappoint. For instance, I am not a gift person at all; I love words. Verbal reassurance and compliments and affirmations make me feel loved, not expensive jewelry.

What makes you feel loved? Is it when people perform acts of service for you or spend time with you? Is it a kiss on the neck? What tangible things or gestures make you feel the most appreciated? Make a long, long list and keep adding to it.

21. **What Are Your Gifts?**

The questions on this list have mostly been inward fac-ing, but we can get just as much joy and satisfaction from recognizing what we can offer the world. Take the time to identify what your gifts are, so you can give and love and serve those around you in the most effective and reward-ing way possible.

And don't tell me you don't have gifts. (You wouldn't dare say that to me after all we've been through, right?) We all have many gifts, and you have beautiful, magnificent ones. But maybe, throughout the years and busyness of life, they have slipped your mind. Luckily, the internet is filled with tools to help change that. Right now, get online and search for the "spiritual gifts test" from Rock Church at sdrock.com. Another must-take is the StrengthsFinder test from Gallup. And there are plenty of others. Take a few! Have fun with it. You are created for a purpose with many gifts, and it's time to let them shine.

So there you go. Twenty-one simple questions. Oh, but quite a few of those aren't so simple to answer, are they? I'll admit that if forty-year-old Dawn Barton had been assigned the "I Love Me" Challenge, she would have labored over it for days, panicking about her identity as she searched through dusty boxes in the attic and old diary entries for answers. Or worse yet, that Dawn might have called the challenge a waste of time and skipped the whole thing. Please don't be forty-year-old Dawn. Accept the challenge and take your time. Sit with each one for a few days; enjoy rolling the possibilities around in your mind. And if you find a particular question difficult, then that's all the more reason to find an answer for it.

Five

The Black Hole of 45+

You're the Best Demographic of Them All

*O*ne day about three years ago, I was happily sitting on my white slipcovered sofa with my favorite faux-fur blanket draped over my crisscrossed legs. My laptop was perfectly nestled in the middle, and I was ready to go through my emails. As I was scrolling I came across an online survey related to a product I was interested in. It was one of those surveys that asks all kinds of questions about your life, what you do, your hobbies, and so on. As I scrolled down, it asked me to check the age that applied to me. Here were the options:

- 18–25
- 25–35
- 35–45
- 45+

What?

My age wasn't even worth mentioning. It felt as if they thought, *Oh, she's in* that *age group. No need to market to her; she'll be dead soon.* I sat on it, mulling it over and over, and the more I thought about it, the more annoyed I got.

I went from a relaxed, fur-wrapped, delicate flower to an enraged imaginary CEO explaining to her board of directors why their idiotic decision to be so dismissive of the ages forty-five-plus would be the very thing that would destroy our organization. During my mental argument with my made-up board of directors, I came up with all the reasons why MY AGE was the most desirable age *to* market to and why we should NEVER be left out of anything.

First, I explained to my board, women drive the majority of all consumer purchasing. We are the best and hottest group of people to sell things to. This is actually a fact.[1] Look at any national earnings report, and we account for more than half of all spending in the US. We control the purse strings of the world, so why does it feel like we're a little forgotten when it comes to marketing, ads, and sales?

Second, I told the board (you should have seen them, their imaginary faces fixed on me with a trembling blend of fear and awe), women talk. We can make or break a product, idea, or person, and you'll never see it coming. Take Spanx, for instance. A woman realized that cutting the feet off her pantyhose solved a hundred different problems and literally became a billionaire. Why? Because women will always tell other women when something makes her skinnier, younger, or less jiggly. It's just how we're wired. Men don't call each other raving about the latest upper-thigh cellulite cream—or any cream for that matter.

Third, we raised the little punk who made up that survey and he should have known better than to disregard his elders.

After my imaginary board meeting ended, I was still worked up. Suddenly, in my mind, the CEO pantsuit was gone and I was an angry Southern mama in a hot kitchen, apron around my waist, with one hand on my hip and the other shaking a wooden spoon as I yelled, "And I'll tell you something else! Don't you ever come in MY house thinking I am not the BEST thing that has ever happened to you. You better respect me right here and now."

You get the picture. In that hot headed couch moment— which was also one of my grandest couch moments of all time—I was determined to prove that we, women my age and beyond, were the most valuable of all. Admittedly, my visceral reaction to this was probably more about my own entering into a season of feeling forgotten. But I needed to prove to myself and to the world why the 45+ group was the greatest marketing demographic in the world.

Needless to say, I didn't finish that survey. Instead, I took my Geritol and spent the day going down a rabbit hole of wondering, *Are we being forgotten? Are we forty-five-plussers getting lumped into one single black hole of vague marketing?*

I started thinking about the women in my life, not the one-off stories you hear about on Buzzfeed or the cover of *Time* magazine, but real women around me.

Take, for instance, my best friend Kali's grandmother, Grandma Deedle. She is a ninety-nine-year-old fireball. She lives her summers in Indianapolis and her winters in Hollywood Beach, Florida, at the top of a high-rise condominium overlooking the Atlantic. She lunches with friends every Friday, plays bridge weekly, has online Zoom sessions with her family and friends, and is active on social media. She has season tickets to the ballet and the symphony, and we all know season tickets mean Grandma Deedle is banking on being around for a while. Oh, and you can join her on any given afternoon for a Jameson on the rocks on the balcony. If the world gave up trying to reach us forty-five-plussers, that would have equated, so far, to more than fifty-four years of spending for Grandma Deedle.

I can assure you there is nothing to pity about this woman, and she is not a demographic to be tossed aside or forgotten. Did you know there are over four million women who are eighty-five-plus in the United States? Did you also know that collectively those women have an income of over $83,767,100,000?[2] I'm no marketing genius, but I'm thinking that when a group of women have over $83 billion, maybe I wouldn't *forget* them. Granted, Grandma Deedle's life may not be the norm, but she is living life, frequenting restaurants and grocery stores. Her season tickets support her city's cultural centers, and she's spending money on clothes, shoes, and certainly her Jameson. I'm just saying, y'all better not forget Grandma Deedle.

At the age of fifty-eight, my sweet friend Viki Weir, along with her daughter Courtney, opened the doors to what may be the single greatest gift store in the world, Pizzaz, in Gulf Breeze, Florida. I have spent more money and time in that store than I should ever admit (I suspect my shopping has paid the rent at their store more than once), and I can recall only a handful of times that Viki wasn't working, even in her seventies. Today she is seventy-three and is still a beautiful bundle of vibrant energy. She's always stylish and always looks amazing, from her clothes to her fabulous lashes. So if Viki, who is herself a walking billboard for whatever brand she's wearing that day, co-owns and buys for one of our town's most popular stores, she's among the most influential women in the area. Marketers would be fools not to pay more attention to her.

Okay, let's look at one woman who wasn't in my own personal circles, Kane Tanaka. In April 2022, Tanaka died at the age of 119. In 2019 a ceremony was held to celebrate her officially becoming the oldest person alive. After the presentation of a certificate and flowers, someone handed Ms. Tanaka a box of fancy chocolates, and without hesitation, she popped one straight in her mouth (as any good woman would).[3] Right there in front of those Guinness World Records officials, a film crew, the audience, and her family. So it seems to me she would be a darn good person to market to if you owned a chocolate company. I mean, a girl can consume a lot of chocolate in seventy-four years (if we assume they stopped marketing to her at forty-five), so why would any company quit marketing to this demographic?

The good news is the little punk who wrote that pathetic survey question might soon find himself out of a job. I'm thrilled to share that the world is starting to wise up a little because, let's be real, money talks. According to AARP, the fifty-plus market contributed more than $8.3 trillion to our economic market, and fifty-six cents of every dollar spent in the United States in 2018 was from someone over fifty.[4] That's more than half! Businesses and the media have started to take notice.

Companies like Anthropologie and J. Crew are targeting our age for part of their product lines, not only with an increase in their size range but also through the styles they offer. You can see in their stores and marketing campaigns that they are listening to our cries for fashion that is designed for our ages. They understand that we don't necessarily want Daisy Dukes and crop tops, but just because we are over forty-five does not mean we want to wear pearls and twin sweater sets either.

Networks are creating shows to target us too. An obvious example might be the *Sex and the City* reboot, *And Just Like That* (too bad it turned out to be a bit of a stinker). We have to celebrate that, when the show debuted at the end of 2021, gorgeous Carrie Bradshaw and her stylish New York besties were about the *same age* that Blanche, Dorothy, and Rose were when the *Golden Girls* debuted.

Okay, so that one isn't the greatest example of this older-women trend because its first season kind of bombed. The writers failed to take into account that in twenty-five years, *SATC* fans like me had matured quite a lot. The scandalous stories we once found so entertaining in our twenties now make us cringe when we see them playing out with women our age because, like I said, we grew up.

But right now you can scroll any of the streaming services and find expensively made shows featuring beautiful women with wrinkles and gray hair in diverse, interesting, sometimes-funny, sometimes-dramatic, compelling lead roles. You'll notice I described the shows as expensive. This is because, while I can't yet vouch for how good they are or will be (I'm still recovering from the disaster that was *SATC* Season 1), one look at the stellar casting and high-production quality tells you that somebody is spending big money on our demographic.

⸺

Even in the grocery store, you'll see that the forty-five-plus crowd is taking up increasing space around us. In the last year or so,

Vogue had three women over age forty-five on their covers, and sixty-one-year-old Paulina Porizkova has appeared in Laura Geller cosmetics ads talking about how she will NOT be forgotten. See, it's a thing, even for supermodels.

So why am I giving you this glorified sales pitch on the joys of being forty-five-plus? Why am I showing you statistics, dollar figures, and examples of supermodels? For a few reasons.

First, because I want you to know that this is yet another way in which you are immensely valued and important. Heck, I'd say you are a part of the most powerful, most sought-after marketing group in the history of the world. Nobody has more purchasing power than your second-half-of-life demographic. Of course, you are a precious child of God and will always be treasured more than our small human minds can understand. But I hope these numbers and these examples remind you that you have influence and agency right here and right now. I want you to be deliberate about recognizing your value and power.

Second, I want to encourage you to use that power. The world is listening and wants to know what you want—everything from shoe designers to salons to cosmetic companies to food. Like I have said, this is not the time to be silent and sit back. This is the time to roar. Support brands and stores that *see* us and try to meet our needs. If you're still in the workforce, make noise about these numbers; help your company recognize the opportunity here. If you've been considering launching your own business aimed at your peers but were afraid that an enthusiastic consumer base wasn't there, think again!

There are people out there staying up late at night trying to design a new gadget, jacket, workout gear, kitchen appliance, and who-knows-what-else with YOU in mind. God help her, but yes, there's some twenty-five-year-old girl out there trying to figure out what makes a forty-five-plus woman happy. Now, you and I both know the answer to that is elastic, but we'll let her keep exploring.

Third, I want to caution against the mindset we saw in that survey. As I talk about throughout this book, it's easy to look back and think it was only in the younger years when we mattered, that we have to fit into a smaller, more scrutinized demographic to have a voice. It's just not true. (And have I mentioned it makes bad business sense?) Until the surveys start to break up the second-half age group as carefully as the first, let us check that forty-five-plus box with pride. It's the gateway to the biggest, most powerful demographic there is.

And most importantly, remember, it's fine to don your CEO cap and lecture your imaginary board from time to time. Let 'em have it.

No One Puts Baby in a Corner

Create a Confident Self-Image

*A*s sure as the sun's glowing rays dance on our faces and sweet, wet Southern air permeates our lungs, so will the savory flavorings of Cajun cooking delight my every emotion. Where I come from, this is who we are. Food is life. Next to God, it's the answer for just about everything; it's like duct tape for us, only better. Feeling blue? Not to worry, we have a crawfish étouffée for that. Stressed? We have a King Cake from Keller's in Lafayette that will sugar away your every worry. Happy? Then let's celebrate with boiled crawfish and Mawmaw's bread pudding.

When you hail from a long line of Cajuns, this is the way things are. It would never occur to any of us to dip into a long, relaxing bubble bath or apply deep-breathing exercises to activate

49

our parasympathetic nervous systems. (I had to look that one up because, as you can see, all I know is to heat up a bowl of jambalaya.) Food has been my magic pill and my comforting blankie for fifty glorious years. The only problem with that little magic pill of mine is that it comes a-callin' with its little friends, remorse and self-loathing. And that remorse and self-loathing tend to stay around long after the leftovers get tidied into the Tupperware.

I have battled with my weight for as long as I can remember. I don't recall a single moment, except during pregnancy, that I looked into the mirror at my body and was pleased with what I saw. Not one. It brings tears to my eyes to even type these words, and I can't help but wonder how something so seemingly easy to resolve could dominate a person's life for so long.

All three of my pregnancies were like a beautiful release; I felt the weight of a thousand disappointments lift away, and for nine months I was free. It didn't matter what number that scale offered up to me because, honey, I was growing a baby! Pregnancy is the only time in a woman's life when society doesn't judge if she eats a box of warm Krispy Kreme donuts, a tub of Blue Bell ice cream, and half a bag of Cheetos all in one sitting. After all, she's eating for two. (Oh hush. I'm well aware that the second person only needs, like, eight calories a day.)

The funny thing is, in giving myself that freedom and permission to not care about my weight, I didn't gain any. I never gained more than fifteen pounds with any of my pregnancies and always weighed less after my daughters were born. However, you'll be thrilled to know I am an overachiever and gained all of it back, and then some, once those babies arrived. Just between us, I weigh more today than the day I went in to deliver my ten-pound, fourteen-ounce daughter, Makenzie. Food for thought.

This battle with my weight, this perpetual awareness that my body isn't what it should be, has always been with me. When I was twelve, I asked my mom to take me to Weight Watchers for the first time. I wanted to go because, even at twelve, I was keenly aware that my body was larger than my friends' at school and I hated it. Was I also a foot taller than everyone else and fully developed into the body of a twenty-five-year-old? Yes. But all I saw was that I was bigger than they were. The fear I felt getting publicly weighed every week is as real to me today as it was more than thirty years ago. I loathed that scale and every scale since then. I hated its truths and its lies: a truth that there was more weight on me than there should be, and a lie that I wasn't enough because of the number that scale produced.

Since you're probably wondering: my mother was especially encouraging because she had struggled with weight for most of her life as well. In some strange way I suspect my being so keenly aware that my body was larger than it should be came from my mother trying so very hard to make sure I did not have to fight the battles that she did. In fact, my mother was so supportive that she decided to make anything and everything sweet in our house with the new, super-fabulous sweetener that had no calories, Sweet'N Low. Everything had this in it. Sweet'N Low coffee, Sweet'N Low tea, Sweet'N Low apple pie, Sweet'N Low shaken all over my grapefruit. Many of my teenage memories are coated in that weird aftertaste. In short, she was incredibly supportive, actually. All of the ladies in my meetings were. I was the only twelve-year-old attending this weight loss group but oddly, I never thought much of that; I guess I just thought I had a mom who fought for me a little harder than most.

From that point in my life, this stupid small contraption on the floor determined my worth. It could tell me every day if I was good or bad, deserving of self-love or not. If the number on the scale was lower, I was a better woman; if it went up, even by one single digit, I was a failure.

I allowed myself to believe that weight was to blame for a multitude of challenges in my life. When I was single and a relationship didn't work, I thought it was because I weighed too much. It definitely couldn't be that I was a pushy, overbearing woman with little to no patience. Nah, it was my flabby arms. I believed if I were thinner, if my body were more toned, if I looked good in a swimsuit, that guy would have called back.

If I weighed less, I would have been more successful, and I would have been a better mother, wife, and friend. That never-attainable lower number on the scale was always the golden ticket to a better life.

I repeatedly replayed my food choices as I laid my head on my pillow at night. I had only egg whites for breakfast and did really well through lunch with my salad and chicken. But then a friend came by and we devoured the freshly delivered all-meat pizza. Why didn't I just stick with coffee? What's wrong with me that I couldn't just have one slice instead of four? Next time she comes, I'll put out grapes. Dinner, oh gosh, dinner. The pasta and the garlic bread. Well, it was only that plate. But then at 9:45 I ate the stinkin' Oreos. Why didn't I just go to bed at 9:30? Was it worth it, Dawn? What's wrong with me? Tomorrow I'll do it right.

It was a forever vicious cycle. Many of my tomorrows did begin with a determination to do better. Often this involved starting the latest and greatest fad diet. Fat-free to full-fat, no fruit to nothing but berries, low-carb living to all-carb Thursdays. Intermittent fasting to ten small meals a day. Eating like a caveman to eating like Daniel before the lions' den. And a heckuva lot of saying to everyone, "It's not a diet; it's a lifestyle change." Thanks to this rich history, I can confidently say I am something of an authority on this area. No one knows more about diets than I do. My battle with weight is NOT for lack of information.

If you know me, I suspect these words may have been a bit of a surprise to you. As women go, I am generally self-assured and even, one might say, overconfident on occasion. But this doesn't take away my reality of a lifelong battle with my weight. Even as a textbook alpha woman, I have not lived fully. I have pulled back and allowed the chains of a scale to dictate events I would attend and people I would spend time with. That insidious number on the scale was my keeper and captor for so, so long.

Nothing ever changes overnight, but sometimes we can recognize turning points, and a pivotal moment in this lifelong battle came about ten years ago when my sister Jodie invited my family to their ranch in the Texas Hill Country for Easter. The place was a visual splendor and looked nothing like my idea of a ranch at all. There was no tumbleweed or dry dirt, and I couldn't see a single cowboy walking around in chaps with a gun on his hip. Heck, there wasn't even a cow or a horse or a saloon in sight. But nonetheless, it was called The Ranch. A 1,600-acre property that had been passed down through generations, it was surrounded by tall hills on every side as if to hide the secret between them. The main house sat by a crystal-clear river, where ziplines and paddleboards awaited you. A guest house was just up a hill with streams of water trickling by its front porch. There was a tennis court, a mini golf course, an outdoor chapel, and so much more. To this day, it is one of the most magnificent places I have ever seen.

But even with all the beauty wrapped into my sister's

invitation, I was hesitant to go. The weather was warm, and in Texas that meant shorts and tank tops. No pants to disguise my legs, no long sleeves to conceal my upper arms, and swimsuits, well, we all know they keep no secrets. But it was family, and I desperately wanted to see Jodie, so we went. Plus it's a little hard to explain to your immediate family that you're canceling their Easter trip because Mommy feels fat.

I was so glad I went. The moment we turned onto the hidden winding road, I felt my muscles let go and relax. Before long, I was with Jodie. Our laughs were constant and the conversations never-ending. A few days into our trip, she and I were walking and talking, and I began sharing my disappointment about my weight and my ongoing struggles. I don't recall how the conversation came up, but I do remember vividly what her response to me was.

"I bet it breaks God's heart to see your body so unhealthy and your heart hurting so much about it."

Those words entered my body like little knives. My initial reaction was to throat punch her and tell her, "Nothing about me makes God sad, you skinny little—" But I didn't. I listened, I hated it, and I soaked it in. Those words hurt so much because of the heaviness of their truth. God never wanted this for me, and I knew it. And just like that, I went home, surrendered my body to God, and I dropped fifty-seven pounds over the next six months.

Okay, not really.

You know God loves growing us through the journey, and goodness knows I have grown so much. In those next six to twelve months, I actually continued to gain a little more weight. My body wasn't going the direction I wanted. But much to my surprise, my mind was. Call it the Jodie Epiphany or the wisdom that comes with age, but the scale's hold on me began to loosen. I decided to embrace the struggle. I don't mean that I decided to give up and start having Coke and fried chicken for breakfast, but I did decide to flip the story in my head. Rather than continually begging God to take away the struggle, the addiction to food, the relentless self-loathing over my body, I decided to thank God for it.

Wait, what?

Now hold on there, firecracker, don't roll your eyes. Hear me out.

What if we are meant to embrace the struggle? I mean really embrace it so much that we are genuinely thankful for it? It took me about a year of wrestling with that brief conversation at the ranch, but eventually my mind began settling into a position of gratitude. I wrote down these simple words and prayed over them daily:

"Thank You for my battles with weight because it gives me a heart for understanding others with this battle. Help me to love myself and my body and to know I am worthy because You made me. Please heal my addiction and replace my desire for food with my desire for You."

That was it. Just three simple lines that I looked at every single day.

When I could authentically and purely thank God for my struggles, it changed everything. During that time I was leading a team of women in Mary Kay, and I began to notice that I had several amazing, vibrant, but *large* women on my team. These women were beautiful and driven and, best of all, a ton of fun! I believe that their time in Mary Kay and specifically with me was a blessing for them and me. God gave these ladies a leader who saw them as so much more than their size but also understood that their weight was a part of them they didn't want to ignore. We could move seamlessly from a whiteboard session on strategy to a heart-to-heart about struggles with worldly standards of beauty, and then back to a spreadsheet on that quarter's sky-high targets. I realized then that God had given me a gift: my pain had become my purpose. I could empathize, and I could push. Together we exemplified the truth that our bodies should have no bearing on our ambition.

We are not a number on a scale, and it is imperative for our own happiness and for the glory of God that we do not allow that little number to dictate our worth.

So let's try something.

Close your eyes. Okay, not really because you can't read this if you do. But after you finish this paragraph, I want you to close your eyes and think about the people you love. Think about the ones who make your heart swell at the very thought of them. The ones whose hugs can make the rest of the world disappear for a moment. The ones who make you laugh or feel beautiful, the ones who lovingly mentored and guided you through life. Can you see them, can you feel what it is to be in their presence? Is there a smile coming across your face? Now hold that in your mind for just as long as you like.

I bet you didn't once think about their weight, did you? Not once.

What if *you* are that person for others? People love you for who you are and how you make them feel. It's not about your waist size or shoe size or any other external, self-imposed physical issue by which you deem yourself to be less-than. It's about you, the wholeness and magnificence of the glorious YOU and all that you are.

Now, on the flip side, we have to stop using our weight as a crutch or a scapegoat. If we feel hurt by people who don't seem to want to spend time with us or who aren't investing in our relationships, we have to take a good, honest look at why. I'm going to rip the Band-Aid off right now, so get ready. If someone doesn't want to be around you, it's not because of your weight, or any of those external things; it's probably because of the way you make them feel when they are in your space. People want to be around those who make them feel good, inspired, happy, and listened to. If your time with others is spent criticizing or judging, or monopolizing conversation, or being self-defeating, people might not want to be around you. It might be hard to hear, but it's true.

So be nice. But also try to be confident and comfortable in your own skin—and when you're not feeling it, fake it till you feel it. Take a deep breath, smile, stand up straighter, and remind yourself that, no matter what you might be feeling about yourself, God is looking at you with pride.

What we are drawn to, or not drawn to, in people isn't their size, at least most of the time. An exception might be the way I'm drawn to Chris Hemsworth in a pair of jeans with his shirt off. Maybe that is a little about his size, but, like, have you seen *Thor*? That situation right there brings me joy . . . but not a deep-down, soulful joy. I'm just kidding, it totally does. But I digress.

From here on out, I want you to let go of the idea that your size equals your appeal to others. It's a heavy burden to carry, thinking that you are less-than because of something physical. I would love to tell you that my body is now the perfect size, but it isn't. However, I did lay down the weight (pun totally intended) of carrying the negative feelings of it. Ironically, in doing so, I became better about what I ate and I began to exercise and move more than I have in the past, which, let's be honest, didn't take much given that my big workout of the day was checking the mailbox.

The difference for me happened in my heart and my mind, and I know it can for you too. My weight doesn't hold me back from going places, or seeing people, or loving that woman I see in the mirror every day. Do I still struggle with my weight? Yes, and perhaps I always will. I understand that life is made up of big battles and little ones; some are temporary and some are lifelong. It's all part of the journey.

I hope my story becomes a breakthrough for you. I pray that as you read these words, you decide to leave that heaviness here. Just drop it right here and turn the page. From this moment forward, there's no more holding back from living life fully. Who cares if we wobble like a bowl of Jell-O when we walk? No one. We need you—all of you. Because you, my friend, are a magnificent blessing to this world at any size.

Seven

Hello, Young Grasshopper

Revel in the, Uh, "Metamorphosis" of the Female Form

I wonder: If someone had handed me a book thirty-five years ago filled with stern warnings of chin hairs and rolled-up breasts, would I have believed a word of it? Probably not.

Thirty-five years ago I was eighteen years old and graduating from Jenks High School with a 1.87 GPA (that's a story for another day). I was fearless about the future and never gave aging a second thought. I suppose if asked, I would have said I was unconcerned because by the time I was to become really old, like in my thirties, there would be a laser that scanned my body and miraculously repaired everything. It would fix broken bones, cancer, and most definitely the crepey lines of aging. I wasn't worried one bit, *and*

I also knew everything. (You can see how that GPA might be tied into my thinking there.)

I'd like to go back in time and have a talk with that young girl. She wouldn't listen because, again, she knew everything, but if I could, I'd tell her a few things.

First, move more, and exercise regularly. My hope is she'd establish some good habits that my older self could maintain—like opting for an occasional walk rather than another bag of Doritos whenever boredom strikes.

Second, I would tell her that this is the only time she will ever be able to wear a tube top and trust that it will stay where it's supposed to be. In the not-so-distant future, those things that were keeping that cute top in place will be resting closer to her waist in complete defeat from their short-lived battle against gravity. I always wanted to wear a tube top and completely missed the window. It's one of my great life regrets.

But most of all, I would tell her that her body, that eighteen-year-old body, is the best it'll ever be, and that now is an excellent time to run around naked. Just run. Let it all hang out because it's smooth and firm and does not ripple for twenty seconds after poking it like a mattress-wave on your cool aunt's waterbed in the eighties.

And when she shops for bathing suits, she should leap past the tankinis and go straight for the thongs because, yes, that butt is firm enough to hang out to all of the world. And then I'd reiterate that she should forget the swimsuit, and just be naked. All the time. She should move to Europe where people commonly go to beaches topless and let EVERYONE see just how perky she is. She should strut everywhere and jump often just to show onlookers that everything still stayed in place. Then, she should go home and just look at herself in the mirror and say "DANG, DAWN!" and "SHUT THE FRONT DOOR, YOU HOT THING" over and over.

But it never works that way, does it? We rarely get the wisdom of knowing when something is so good that we should, for instance, run around naked. We are so wrapped up in what we aren't or how different we are from another person that we miss the "Wow, I'm amazing!" moments. And about the time we figure out just how darn good IT was, IT is gone and in its place are two breasts that have to be rolled up like sleeping bags to fit back in that eight-year-old bra.

I, like most women, completely missed the firm-body celebratory years because I was too busy worrying about things like getting my hair perfectly feathered back like Farrah Fawcett or recreating Madonna's leather-jacket-and-fishnet-tights look. By the time my late twenties were upon me, it was too late. I was starting to see the first signs of what would be my body's refusal to age gracefully. In the most puzzling way, the hairs on my eyebrows and eyelashes started to navigate their way to my chin. What was particularly perplexing about this was that I could only see those hairs if I was in a car with someone (usually a date) or on my way to a very important social event and there wasn't a tweezer within a ten-mile radius.

Of course, I shouldn't have been surprised by those first mortifying chin hairs. I had long suspected there was some genetic man mutation for the women in my family. Once, when I was thirteen, I heard my grandmother tell my mom that she was going in for surgery and my mother better bring the tweezers to the hospital. "I need you to pluck my upper lip and chin if I'm out of it for a few days," she said. My grandmother was VERY serious about this;

there were to be no wild facial hairs. So I knew this sort of thing existed. But I didn't know how bad it was going to get.

I remember being completely smitten with a man when I was about twenty-eight; we will call him Lee. I'm changing his name to protect my ego. One day, we were lying down, facing each other and kissing. (Yes, gasp, I kissed other men before my husband.) At some point, I rolled onto my back to look at the ceiling and bask in the gloriousness of this tender moment. Then Lee said, "Wait, you have a hair on you." He reached toward a spot about three inches down from my collarbone and tried dusting it away. I thought nothing of it until his brow furrowed in confusion. Then he grabbed the hair between his thumb and pointer finger and tugged. I felt a sharp pull and I knew. That was no stray hair. It was part of my man growth and that sucker was attached. He tugged gently several times, as if in disbelief that a woman would ever have a hair there—and certainly not one this long and thick. His face was filled with a mix of horror and disbelief that the hair could possibly be attached. It was. In that moment, a piece of me died. Just flat-out died.

This might surprise you, but Lee and I did not make it. He says it was for other reasons, but I can't help but wonder how much that man-hair played into it.

For two decades, I heard neither hide nor hair (sorry, but it had to be said) of this unexpected bodily betrayal outside of my own family. It was a shame-filled secret I was willing to take to the grave. Then, thankfully, in my midthirties I began to observe other women admitting to hair growth in unwanted places. I was elated, because if you're a girl growing a goatee, it's better to have some other goatee-growing women around you for moral support and all.

But must we women go months, if not years, wondering if

we're the only ones witnessing the chaos on our bodies? We waste countless hours agonizing about the stray man-hairs because no one warned us it was coming. Why aren't mature women sharing this knowledge generation to generation, helping to mentally prepare the youthful hotties of what's to come? I think it's time for us to spread the word. One of those young ladies may discover the solution to one of our many problems, so it's best if we start telling them now.

I know it's a tad late for this one, but my first step will be issuing a long-overdue warning to my younger self. Feel free to tear this out, change the names, and hand this to the unsuspecting young women in your life.

Dear eighteen-year-old Dawn,

If you know me, and I think you do, you know I believe that there are many gifts in life and none of us gets all of them. We each get some, and that's the way it's supposed to be. I also think that this should be the case when it comes to aging—nobody gets all the . . . let's call them "features of maturity" . . . and we all get some. But oh, young me—as far as I can tell, you're gonna get them ALL.

Let's start at the top—our hair.

The good news, young Dawn, is that your hair is going to continue to be one of your favorite traits. It will stay lush and sexy and behave appropriately in almost all types of weather. At the age of fifty-three, you'll only have about ten to twelve grays, thank you Jesus. But it will begin thinning. How do I know? Ten years ago my ponytail holder could only be wrapped around my hair twice, but now it can wrap around three times. Don't tell us a 1.87 GPA girl can't do science.

Your hair will also move. It will fall out of your head, brows, and lashes, and show up in other places where you don't expect it. As I write this, my eyebrows have all but disappeared except for this little patch that resembles the mustache of Hitler right in the center of what used to be a full brow that arched beautifully over each eye. My eyelashes have given up on growing end to end, much like my eyebrows. But not to worry because my upper lip and my chin have nearly filled in to create a full goatee.

All that money you're spending to get rid of hair on your body will start going toward *keeping* your hair when you're older. Your brows will be microbladed, your lashes will drip with serums that promise length and volume—and that's just to make them sturdy enough to hold fake lashes. One day the idea of a clip-in hair extension won't sound so bad because you'll feel convinced it'll make you look exactly the way you do today. At 53, we haven't done this yet but we're very open to it. On the flip side, your showers will get shorter and you'll buy fewer razor blades because your hair *down there* starts thinning and turning into a reverse mohawk of sorts and the hair on your legs just kind of gives up for months at a time.

May I also add, your forties might be a very good time to try to take a plastic surgeon as a lover. A fling with someone who stocks collagen will really help out financially. (Karen, I'm just teasing. Breathe.)

Your skin. Now this is a biggie, mostly because your youthful mind cannot possibly wrap itself around the phenomenon that awaits. Your skin will throw in the towel on its decades-long fight against gravity. On every part of your body, it's going to seek a nice low area to lie down and rest—your face, chest, arms, and knees . . . everywhere. But it will be ever so slight and sneaky. You won't notice anything for years and then one day you'll be trying on a polka-dot bathing suit at Target and you'll catch sight of yourself in the three-way mirror and realize the cheeks of your butt have drifted so far south that you could carry a can of Coke under each one. Of course, you could also stick a Coke can under both breasts, grab a can in each hand, and tell people you have a six pack. See, there's always a silver lining.

Young, taut Dawn, you'll feel like Elastigirl (ooh—you don't know about Pixar yet, do you? Animated movies are about to get a lot more interesting), except your skin never comes back after being stretched; it just stays there, getting comfy in its new spot. It also holds grudges and remembers every single time you drenched it in baby oil and basked in the sun—especially the days you used reflective foil to enhance your chances of skin cancer. In the future, you'll go outside covered head-to-toe in SPF 50 and you'll still return indoors with little markings on your skin. It's as if your skin is sending some code to say, "I'll never forget what you did to me." These are called age spots. They are not freckles, no matter what you tell yourself.

You'll have perpetual bags that even the toughest eye creams cannot minimize. Your eyeballs will start to disappear under your napping eyelids. Those middle lashes you have left will make a noble effort to hold that sagging skin like a strong man at a circus lifting hundreds of pounds on his barbell, but you're going to have to help them out at some point. You will decide to "get your eyes done," and at first you'll feel nervous and a little guilty, but you shouldn't. A Dr. LeBeau will do an amazing job at fixing them, and it will be one of the best gifts you've ever given yourself. For the record, you will not take Dr. LeBeau as a lover mostly because you adore his wife and your own husband.

(Let me cut in here to say the procedure took an hour and a half, I was wide awake for it, and was out and about two days later. I look ten years younger and it did wonders for my confidence. If you've been on the fence about it, you have my vote to go for it. I'm a fan of doing whatever you want that makes you feel better. Well, not like crack or anything, but a little Botox and a nip and tuck? Sure. Okay, back to my letter . . .)

We also need to talk about your neck. The neck situation is especially sneaky and might slip past you for years because you're so accustomed to viewing yourself straight on in the mirror. But trust me. Sometime in, say 2017, check out your profile. See the way the skin drapes like a curtain from your chin to your larynx? Yeah, you too will get the "turkey neck" you've been hearing about your whole life. But the nice thing about it is I'm fairly certain it's linked to all the laughing you've been doing through the years.

And God works in mysterious ways. One of the nice things that happens during your transformation is that your vision will also go, so it will become harder to see it all.

You'll become a person who says things like "I just hate to drive at night," and you'll have to lift your head in a weird, awkward position so you can see out of your progressive lenses. Oh, you don't know what progressive lenses are yet, do you? They're lenses with a reading prescription at the bottom and the distance prescription at the top, and if you're lucky, somewhere in the middle you'll be able to see things.

Sigh, what else? Your feet will get bigger, your toenails will get thicker, and you'll start buying shoe inserts to support your arches. Tolerance for loud noises plummets while, ironically, you have to ask people to speak up. Your memory and word recollection also go downhill. You'll initially blame that on cancer. (Oh gosh, you don't know about the cancer yet, do you? Don't worry, it'll be the best thing that happens to you, I promise. Another benefit: cancer treatment is the reason you never go through any weird menopause stuff, so you'll have to ask someone else about that.) But you'll eventually find that when you sit with girlfriends your age, everyone else is repeating the same stories too.

Before I wrap up, let's go back to the naked thing. (I hope you're naked and jumping as you read this.) Enjoy the way you can eat what you want and nothing happens to your body, because one day—you won't know when—that superpower will come to a screeching halt. Somewhere between your upper arms and your thighs, there will be an extra fifteen pounds (or fifty in my case) that just stays for the rest of your life. It's like it claims squatters' rights and nothing—I mean nothing—will get it to leave. (But don't worry, eventually you'll realize that your efforts to lose them are making you unhappy and instead you'll come to love those squatters.)

So there you have it, young grasshopper; now you know. Your body will age and at times it will feel like it is fighting you and betraying you. It's not an easy thing to watch. But remember that same body is wondrous and beautiful. It can stretch and make tiny humans, it can fight off cancers, and it can mend hearts that have been broken.

The wrinkles and scars of a life well lived are not things to be ashamed of, and you don't have to hide them. Although you don't have to feel guilty about trying to hide them. Goodness knows I am not going gently into that good night and am actively fighting these wrinkles every step of the way. To date I've had Botox on my crows' feet and the elevens (but not on my forehead because for some reason beyond my understanding I don't wrinkle there . . . yet). I've also had fillers (I mean, the sides of my mouth started to cave in and my upper lip just started disappearing), and you already know about my eyes. But please know you are not less of a woman or less beautiful because you no longer look eighteen.

My last piece of advice: on July 17, 1998, do a quick tweezer check on your chest before Lee comes over.

Love,

Fifty-three-year-old Dawn

PS: When I was in my forties, I formed a theory about why our level of hotness starts to fade as we get older: We are like packages. When we're young, we need to sell it with a gorgeous wrapper because there's not so much on the inside.

But now, in my early fifties, I realize I was wrong on two accounts. First, young Dawn, you did already have so much inside you. And I don't just mean your legendary metabolism. Second, yes, what's inside our older selves is *so* good—we've cultivated some stunning inner beauty by now—but on top of that, we finally get that what's on the outside doesn't determine our identity and value. It's not crucial to our sense of self. And boy, is there a lot of freedom in that.

Eight

Hail to the No

Learn to Say No and Define What YOU Want

There is a massive, invisible racetrack in life. It's long but not oval in shape like the ones around our high school football fields. Instead, this racetrack is a little more like a slightly curved line, and it expands so far into the horizon that it is impossible for us to ever see the finish line. The track is made up of an infinite number of lanes divided by white lines, each measuring about four feet in width. As women, we are lovingly placed on that track in our own special lane by our parents, and the world around us reinforces that we stay in it. And not knowing any different, we run, and we run, and we run on the racetrack of life.

We stay in our own specific lane, being the best versions of ourselves we can possibly be, while briefly stopping along the way to pick up the additions of life: friendships, education, marriage, children, careers, hobbies. Sometimes we don't stop and life tosses more stuff at us anyway. Slowly, slowly, bit by bit, our load gets a little larger and heavier, with some things we desire and some we don't. And generally speaking, we do an incredible job carrying it all and staying in our lanes as we run that race.

But one day the weight of it feels heavier than ever before, and the distance we have traveled begins to wear on our feet. Our backs start to ache and we simply tire of carrying it all. That's when, for the first time, we notice that our lane is actually lined with benches. Lots of benches. And the longer we run, the more inviting those benches become. One day we slow down and decide to stop and have a seat on a bench—but only for a moment.

And in that tiny reprieve, we decide that, just for a moment, we will place the many things we're carrying on the ground next to our feet. We lean back, close our eyes, and breathe. We breathe a long, deep breath as if trying to coax the oxygen from our nose to our fingertips and toes. Once it feels as if that breath has reached the outermost parts of our very being, we begin to exhale.

This is more than a simple act of carbon dioxide leaving our bodies. As our lungs move inward and push the air out of our bodies, it pushes something else out too—all the unnecessary confines of our lives. The "you have tos," the "you shoulds," and the "because it's always been done that ways." And in that moment, sitting on an imaginary bench along an imaginary track, we make a decision to start saying NO to carrying it all.

Imagine that. Visualize it. See yourself transported to the No Zone.

The No Zone is a magnificent place to arrive in one's life. It's empowering and freeing. It's where you finally start saying no to carrying the things you are *supposed to* carry rather than the things you *want* to carry. You step into a life where you are saying yes to YOU and to all that gives you a better and happier life. You begin reaching for the bars that YOU set, not bending to societal demands that don't sit right with you. I don't mean you're riding off a cliff in some impetuous Thelma and Louise moment. (Or maybe you are; I guess it all depends on where you're coming from, but can I request metaphorical cliffs only?) Either way, I know one thing: there is enormous freedom in one tiny word, and it's time for us to embrace it even more.

The No Zone is where you say NO.

Okay, sure, maybe I have a little bit of a flair for the dramatic, but I am here to tell you that when you cross that point in your life—that "I really don't care what you think" line—it's like putting on a Superman cape and dropping twenty-two pounds all at the same time. It's a remarkable feeling, and I highly recommend it.

I have to admit, I thought I was in the No Zone waaaay before I actually was. I've always been pretty good at saying no to things I knew I didn't want to do, so I smugly believed I'd been sitting on one of those benches for years, confidently controlling how I wanted to use my time and energy. Dawn, can you bring home-made cupcakes to the second grade Valentine's Day party? Nope. I'll stop by Publix on the way. Can you volunteer to help take down the stage after church? No, but I am happy to ask my young, strong child to do so. But she might say no too. Can you come out with us to the grand opening of the new wine bar downtown? No, I'm going to bed at 8 p.m. with Ben, Jerry, and the staff of *Downton Abbey*.

But guess what? It turns out that some of my difficulty in

saying no was about acquiescing to demands I hadn't even realized were demands. They were expectations so ingrained in what the world expected of me as a professional woman that I never paused to consider whether I wanted to meet those expectations.

My big bench moment occurred in a rather unexpected and peculiar way—in my house, and because of social media. When it was time for my first book to be released, it was important, according to my publisher and my agent, for me to focus on increasing my social media following. I needed a more authentic approach, really showing "me" so that readers would resonate more easily. More engaged followers would translate into a stronger community (yay for me) and more sales (yay for everyone who needs to make money from my book). Sure, that made perfect sense— except for one part. I was ridiculously self-conscious about the way I looked on camera. Everything I had done up to that point involved carefully written posts and an edited, perfectly posed photo on a highly curated feed.

If I were to just "be myself," then the world would see that I rarely wore makeup and that I have what used to be a respectable double chin that was rapidly morphing into a hanging-swaying back-and-forth kind of chin. *Okay, sure,* I thought. *It'll be fine if I could place the camera just so, face it straight-on, and stay perfectly still because any amount of movement would set off neck reverberations for several seconds at a time.* But I was born to use my hands and my entire face when I speak. Also, I think talking and staying completely still at the same time are physically impossible. You can see the problem.

But I started making the videos, and as long as I had a good hour to get my makeup perfected and I'd avoided all caffeine to keep myself as unmoving as possible, they were okay. Then, one day, in a rush to get something posted and out the door, I quickly posted a video, a BAD one—without filters or makeup, and even a moment when I looked over my shoulder and gave the world a profile shot that revealed my melting mess of a neck.

And you know what?

Nothing happened. No one cared. Not a single "are you sure you intend to be recording right now?" comment. Because when it came down to it, people weren't following me for strategies on how to get a tighter neck or makeup tips.

So I took a day and really dove into it. Who is Dawn Barton and what message do I want to send out into the world through this crazy thing called social media? Was it one of perfectly coiffed hair and makeup, and a perfectly filtered curated feed that screamed, "You are less if these things aren't perfect"? Heck no. I wanted to be a person who helped make another woman's day a little bit better. I wanted to be a friend and share joy and hope and goodness. None of those things needed to be wrapped up in the flawlessness of extreme social media filters.

So I said *no* to looking perfect on camera, *no* to perfectly curated feeds, *no* to anything that wasn't real. And you know what? The number of followers started to increase.

When we become more authentic about who we are and even a little more vulnerable, it's like honey to a bear for other women. We are so drawn to one another's authenticity, we can't even help ourselves. We want to know that we aren't alone, that someone else has the same struggles and joys that we do. We want to see ourselves in others and to feel connected. Believe it or not, a lot of that comes in saying NO. Because when we keep saying yes to the things that don't make us a better woman, we're sending out the wrong message about what matters to us and what doesn't.

At best, these messages might cause us to miss out on connecting with others as deeply as we could; at worst, we could be perpetuating the same unfair, unrealistic expectations society is placing on all of us.

Once I crossed into the glorious No Zone in my late forties, I began giving permission to myself to say no and set healthier boundaries. It was like I started skipping through my life with a magic wand tapping on all of the different things in my life . . . nope, no way, nada, nein, nevah. I was a fierce superhero with a dazzling NO wand.

No to stiletto heels because they now make my feet and my back hurt. No to staying up late because I really like alone time in the morning. No to gluten because it makes me have explosive diarrhea and my joints hurt. (Hey, some things we should say no to are more obvious than others.) No to going to the grocery store because I HATE it and for me, it's worth paying the $99 a year to have them delivered. No to getting my nails done because it doesn't feel like pampering to me; it feels like torture to sit still in a chair for that long and not use my hands. No to watching the news because I like the way I feel much better when I don't. No to drinking alcohol most of the time, not because I'm not completely delightful when I do, but because I can't ever find three days in my schedule for recovery afterward. I've learned to say no to full, tight schedules because I like a lot of downtime. No to business things that are only about money and not about heart. I've become very good at the nos.

I'd like to tell you that I've said no to carbs and dairy and processed foods, but I am a work in progress and I'm not a machine. Oh, and I've also decided to say no to running. Have I ever gone running before? No. But it's good to have this policy in place should anyone ask.

I could go on and on about all the little things I've decided to say no to, and make no mistake, they add up to some big results filled with freedom and empowerment. But I have also learned to say no to big things. For instance, I have fine-tuned my friendships by learning to say no to the friendships that feel entirely one-sided and leave me feeling like someone took the end of a vacuum cleaner and sucked the very life out of me.

Learning to be great at saying no is a rite of passage in our midlife. If you have not crossed into the No Zone yet in your life, I want to give you full permission to do so. You have given so much of yourself, and it's time to really define and embrace what YOU want. And it's not just about saying no to fancy stilettos and opting for the orthopedic Oofos flip-flops. It's about making a decision that your time, your energy—both mental and physical—and your preferences about how to exist in this world are worthy of being honored and protected.

You deserve a life that you joyfully design and live out, and sometimes that comes through a season of reevaluating. We cannot live a healthy life if it is constantly being lived for others. Of course we are here to love others and bless others, but all that has to come from a healthy core. If you are not defining boundaries for yourself, those who matter to you do not get the best of you. They just get what's left of you.

The older I have gotten the better I am at fine-tuning the no, which also means thinking about what I say yes to. I am learning to ask myself: *Does saying yes serve my purpose, my well-being, my values, my priorities?*

Because what we say no to and what we say yes to are equally important.

～

I have this fabulous and fun friend named Tammy. She's a stunning Southern blonde beauty and has fully embraced the No Zone. For many years she dressed the part of her entrepreneurial lifestyle with the perfect heels and outfits but then retired and decided she was done with it all. She turned in every pair of her fancy high heels for many, MANY pairs of fabulous tennis shoes. All kinds of colors and brands with differing amounts of bling and even animal prints.

I once saw a photo of Tammy attending a wedding where she wore a gorgeous black tunic dripping with strands of pearls over beautiful flowing black pants. Simple, elegant, classy. But as I panned down to the bottom, I saw that Tammy had finished off that runway-sleek outfit with pink and orange Adidas sneakers. I'm not going to lie, my Southern wedding attire snob heart skipped a beat. What on earth was she thinking? Where were her high heels? Or at the very least a low pointed-toe flat?

Well, there's a story behind those sneakers. (You knew there would be, right?) It turns out that the wedding was for the granddaughter of Tammy's dear and precious Aunt Beth. Beth was in her eighties and had a great deal of difficulty walking, so she generally got around in a wheelchair. She was worried she wouldn't be able to attend the wedding because the venue was a little hilly and the paths were gravel, not paved.

So Tammy volunteered to push Aunt Beth's wheelchair, a task that would require strong arms and sure footing. "I know it didn't look good," Tammy said, "but it was more important to me that Beth be able to attend and fully experience that special wedding than it was for me to look pretty." Tammy had said no to what people expected of her appearance so she could say yes to helping this aunt she loved so much.

I admire her so much for it.

This isn't about just wearing comfy shoes; it's about stepping up and saying no to the things that do not serve you well. Please don't read this chapter and believe that it is a permission slip to say no to anything that is hard in your life. Most of the time, the hard things produce the best of things and the juiciest fruit. The difficult things build the most character and make for the very best stories. Most of all, the hard things create seasons where we have to fully push into a relationship with the Lord. And beautiful things always come out of that.

With that in mind, my sweet friend, if you haven't already, step into the No Zone. Sit down on one of those benches and start making a list of all the things you want to say no to. Then pull out that fierce fairy wand on those puppies and say, "No, nope, not gonna do it." You are worth this. You deserve this. Now go say NO.

Nine

Rescue Yourself

Be the Hero of Your Own Story

Hello, my name is Dawn Barton. I write and speak about joy, and I've battled depression most of my adult life. Yep, there you have it. I've had a love-hate relationship with Lexapro, Prozac, Wellbutrin, and plenty of supplements for more than thirty years. So yes, the woman who shouts to the world about unstoppable joy is also the woman about to share her story of depression.

My battles with depression began in my early twenties with the loss of my precious daughter Madison. Three months after her death, my husband and I divorced, neither of us knowing how to cope. Four months later a man broke into my home and I was raped; he was caught and it went to a full jury trial. (It's an incredible story, and you can hear more about it in my first book.) I spent my twenties reeling from the tragedies of my life and dancing around the edge of a black hole of sorrow, doing just about anything to avoid feeling the pain. I was constantly trying to escape through either alcohol and partying or continual social events, anything to not be alone with the pain.

You don't have to have gone through something traumatic to experience this. In the United States, anxiety and depression affect more than forty million adults a year. Yes, either can result from life events, but it can also be due to genetics and brain chemistry.[5] For me, there is a chemical imbalance in my brain. Although I've been through traumatic events that have triggered episodes of deep depression, I've also had it hit out of nowhere when everything in life was going awesome. It's a sneaky and wicked beast.

By the way, in addition to my on-again, off-again struggles with depression, I have attention deficit disorder. I don't mean, *Gosh, I guess I'm a little spacey today,* but more like, *I've just read this paragraph forty-four times and still can't tell you a single thing that's in it.* It's almost impossible for me to read or write without ADD medication—which is a little funny seeing as how I *write* books for a living. Often it's a vicious cycle. There's so much noise in my head that I can't focus on doing anything, so I do nothing, and since I'm doing nothing, the feelings of failure creep in and feed that demon of depression, and when I'm depressed, it's even harder for me to control my ADD.

Depression looks a little different for everyone, but for me it feels like a heavy, dark blanket that rests itself over my entire body. I cry easily. I'm fearful and default to the negative rather than the positive. I get angry easily. (If I find myself continually irritated with my dogs, that is generally a red flag because I love my fur babies.) I don't want to see anyone or go anywhere. I just want to be in my bed watching TV. All. The. Time. And I know that's not me. God did not create me or you to live a life of sadness and fear and to watch countless hours of television. (Except for *Downton Abbey*; He did create time in the day for us to watch that.) We are made to be a light, and depression sucks every bit of that out of me.

While nothing feels lonelier than being stuck in the dark quicksand of depression, the National Institute of Mental Health says that more than twenty-one million people battle with depression. That's massive. But what I really want to talk about is another figure: more than 36 percent of those people never seek treatment.[6]

That means there are over nine million people who are hurting in this way and have no path to escaping it. This breaks my heart.

There are any number of reasons people don't seek help for depression—including financial, cultural, practical, and who knows how many others—but one I'm all too familiar with is the view of mental health within the Christian community.

There is a great debate in the Christian community about medications for depression. People have said that mental illness results from some immorality or sinfulness, that it has spiritual causes, and therefore should be treated through prayer, not medication. Although I agree that every issue—heck, even every non-issue—should be treated with prayer, I do struggle with this because I don't see anyone up in arms about using insulin for diabetes or statins for high blood pressure. Depression is a chemical imbalance in the brain and medication can be a blessing. I have been told so many times that I needed to pray harder or fast more or seek God more, and all of that is true. We all do. But I believe that God calls us to actively pursue being the healthiest humans we can be. Mental health affects everything, and the fact that anyone would ever not seek treatment for healing out of fear of being judged is heartbreaking.

Now, just to be clear, I believe that Jesus can do all things and that God is the *ultimate* healer and physician. He is a miracle worker and I have been the recipient of those miracles more than once. But I also believe He works through people to create things to help us. Imagine a woman who's been working in a lab year after year praying for the wisdom to develop something, anything, that could help her mother who suffers with debilitating anxiety and depression. She's prayed to God every day, pleading for guidance and a miracle. Then, one day she and her team discover that they can help people with depression by increasing the serotonin levels to the brain. Do we think that just because the treatment is classified as a drug God couldn't have had a hand in creating it? I hope not.

If I was diagnosed with cancer again next week, I would fight it with everything available to me. I would take chemotherapy, radiation, and whatever the protocols were to save my life, *and* I would pray fervently. I would never not seek medical help and only pray for my situation. I would add in the protocols that the doctors offered and fervently pray for healing.

For me, antidepressants have worked for many years. Sometimes I needed to take them for just ninety days or so, and other times, like the year of my cancer battle or when I was dealing with the loss of my daughter, the rape, and divorce, I took them for much longer. Through the years, I've ridden on the roller coaster of depression so often that I know its every turn. I know its slow climb to a clouded fog, and I know the thrust of its downward plummet into a darker sadness. It's a ride that can last for years or weeks. But I've also learned to recognize it and try to take the necessary steps to get off while I'm still on the slow climb. Being proactive is key for me—before my behaviors of retreating to the safety of my bed and hiding away from the world begin. The longer I let it go, the harder it is to pull out of. I have to move fast.

Part of moving fast means recognizing positive and negative triggers in my life. I know to pull from the positive list every day and to combat the negative things with the positive ones. For me, my positive list includes things like outdoor time, a walk, music, a candle, lunch with a friend, laughter, and more. My negative list includes cloudy days, overeating, and women who say, "It's not a diet; it's a lifestyle" (I'm just kidding). Memorizing these lists—and adding to them as the years go by—is a part of my arsenal to keep my mental state healthy. And when these stop working and I can't get off the roller coaster on my own, I know to call my doctor.

And honestly, sometimes none of the above seem to work. I can find myself in a funk that hangs on hard and long. It is exhausting. All the moves that usually lift me out of a depression in the past don't work. I can try increasing the dosage on my antidepressant. I can be proactive about getting up and getting out every day, taking lots of walks, showering and wearing makeup—even the occasional sexy red lipstick. But I just can't seem to turn the corner.

Those are the times when I'm more grateful than ever that I've become comfortable talking openly about my struggles with mental health. I need people in my day-to-day orbit who see when I'm drowning inside my own mind, who recognize the signs and can jump in to keep me afloat until that particular bout of depression lifts. Sometimes rescuing yourself means surrounding yourself with lifeguards before you need them.

I am also reminded in those darker times that the solutions currently available aren't perfect and I must be proactive in researching and understanding the emerging and lesser-known means of treating myself. While I am all for taking medication when that is the best option available, I'm also aware that sometimes pharmaceuticals can fail us. For many of us, the path toward healing is winding and undulating, and it's one we might have to walk our entire lives.

Knowing others are on the same path can be immeasurably helpful. That's why it bothers me that we don't talk about this enough. We worry about stigma and discouragement from our churches. We're so busy caring for everyone else, and yet we don't address our own well-being with the same persistence and creativity. If our child or best friend were suffering, we wouldn't stop trying to rescue him or her. Yet when it's the woman in the mirror, we don't see her value and we don't try desperately to save her.

Or sometimes we do, but it takes us awhile. Let me tell you about my friend Reba (not her real name, but isn't Reba a fabulous name?). For as long as she could remember, Reba wanted to be a stay-at-home mom. She wanted to snuggle, nurse, and be physically available 'round the clock for her future babies, like her own mother had. Being a mom was her calling in life—she was certain.

When she first told her new husband this, he almost choked on his Snapple (that's what I picture him drinking in 2008), because he was working a nonprofit job and making very little money. But sure enough, when they had their first baby, Reba left her job.

Fast-forward a few years: Twins plus one more had joined the stay-at-home momming scene. All four kids were (and still are) gorgeous and bright and healthy and funny, and Reba was loving being their mother more than anything in the world.

But also, she was close to imploding.

See, before Reba even had children, she was diagnosed with anxiety and had taken medication on and off for years. Having kids cranked up the anxiety. After the initial high of birthing her first, Reba fell into a funk and often dreaded leaving the house with the baby. When the twins were born, she started taking breastfeeding-safe antidepressants and spent another year on the couch tandem-nursing (which she was proud of) while her toddler watched *Frozen* on repeat (which she was ashamed of). When the fourth baby came along, she tried to skip the antidepressants until she found herself sobbing to her doctor about despair, heart palpitations, insomnia, and breathlessness. He prescribed more meds and it helped—but it didn't change the big picture.

For the record, none of this was evident from the outside looking in. Despite Reba's internal struggles, she and her husband were building a fun, busy, creative, loving world for their kids. Their Instagram life was mesmerizing. You would LOVE to be a child in this family. But for Reba, most of the time, parenting felt relentless and overwhelming.

Nevertheless, by early 2020, things were hitting some sort of stride. The kids were finally all in school or preschool, which meant Reba had some breathing room. The freelance marketing work she had crowbarred into the preceding few years had a chance to flourish a bit. She'd also pursued an old dream of becoming a certified fitness instructor and began teaching classes. She was starting to feel like herself again.

Then Covid hit. The schools closed. Suddenly, all four kids were home again. Reba was expected to not only mother them but to manage their homeschooling while also keeping her freelancing and online fitness class commitments—without a single quiet moment to herself. It wasn't pretty.

Here's a scene Reba described to me, just weeks into lockdown: She was in her basement watching each child at their own desk bumbling through their online schoolwork—losing passwords and chargers, sneaking YouTube videos, fighting over everything. She felt suffocated on the inside, numb, panicked, angry—and before she knew it, she was shouting at her kids without even fully realizing what she was saying. Whatever was coming out of her mouth could only be described as misery. Instead of being the cheerleader she felt her children needed to get through the pandemic, she was wondering how much damage she might do to them.

Meds weren't going to fix this.

But guess what? That's right about when a nearby nonprofit invited Reba to apply for a leadership role. They knew Reba and her freelance work, and the job was likely hers for the taking. Accepting it would mean changing the plan though. It'd mean reconfiguring all the fragile but functioning systems their household had in place. It'd mean enrolling the kids in a not-cheap private school that was operating during Covid. It'd mean Reba being away about nine hours every day.

It meant Reba letting go of that calling to be a stay-at-home mom.

But here's a secret Reba knew: The freelancing she'd managed to squeeze into the corners of her momming life through the years—in the early mornings and late nights, during brief spurts of childcare, or while the kids devoured their iPads—was when she'd felt her calmest. Renewed, invigorated, independent. She loved being a mother, but she loved mothering more when she had time away from it.

She says when she was offered the job, it was "a huge sign from God directly to me that He knew it was best for all of us for me to be free."

She took the job. They enrolled the kids in private school. (It used up most of Reba's paycheck, but was it worth it? *Yes.*) Today, they're still working out the kinks of the new arrangement. Reba still struggles with anger and anxiety, but it feels more manageable now. She says that, although nothing is ever perfect, there's an underlying calm in the home now that everyone spends most of their day in their right place.

She rescued herself, and in doing so she rescued all six people living in that house. (Well, she'd put it this way: "I didn't rescue myself; God threw me a lifeline.")

We must pursue our healing with the same fervor we would for anyone else we love. (Or, if you're Reba, grab ahold of that stinkin' lifeline.) Remember, God can move mountains, but don't be surprised when He throws you the shovel. Every time I hear that saying, I'm reminded that I am called to MOVE. He calls us to fight, take the steps, do the research, and arm ourselves with knowledge AND with Scripture. He calls us to be proactive.

When you are depressed, you have to hold on to what you know. I know God is good. I know I am blessed. I know I will be blessed. I know depression doesn't come from God. I know He brings hope. I know there is hope. But the mind is complex beyond comprehension, and sometimes knowing these things isn't enough. Sometimes it hits you that you can't sit waiting for change to happen to you.

If you have tried one way to heal and it didn't work, try something else. Whatever you do, don't give up. Keep fighting for YOU. Be an active participant in your own rescue.

Girl, Let It All Out

A Little Vulnerability Can
Change Your Life

I'm one of those all-in kinds of people. If I decide I like something, or that there's something I want to try, there's no going slowly and gently feeling my way through. For me it's more like a blonde bull in the proverbial china shop yelling, "I'M HERE, Y'ALL!" I'm passionate about all the things I love: my people, my animals, my places, my food. And I'm extremely passionate about my faith. Now, I wasn't always that way; in fact, I was a believer for a long time before I was a *passionate* believer. I didn't even know you could be all that excited about Jesus. I thought good Christians were reserved, soft-spoken, and super polite. Oh, and they were generally pretty old. Based on the elderly congregations I grew up with, I'd concluded it took many years to get Jesus *all* the way into a person.

My sweet friend Stephanie Payne showed me just how wrong I was. Stephanie and her husband, Tim, founded Momentum, a church in Gulf Breeze, Florida. I came to know them in the beginning stages of their church—about three months in, to be exact. I fell in love with who they were and the excitement of building something new in our town, and I was all in. Now, I will clarify that my version of being "all in" in a scenario like this rarely includes setting things up or taking them down (skills desperately needed in a new church that doesn't have a permanent location) or cleaning things or cooking things—I've never been *that* all in for anything. So in this case my "all-in" status meant I was an excellent hype girl.

I was excited about all the possibilities this church brought to our little city. I loved meeting new people, and the way Tim preached was new to me. Tim was a bold, energetic, and passion-filled pastor—he spoke in a relatable, conversational way, holding my attention with stories about how the Bible's teaching related to our everyday lives; he could make me laugh and bring me to tears in the space of twenty minutes. Prior to attending Momentum, I had attended mostly Catholic churches and one conservative Methodist one, where the pastor and priests—though wonderful in their own ways—were solemn and more prescriptive, with lots of recitation and little spontaneity. This more contemporary way of sharing Jesus excited me.

What does any of this have to do with vulnerability? Hold on, I promise I'm getting there.

Early on, Momentum introduced a program of community groups, creating a way to connect people within the church, to invite outsiders in, and to, well, love on one another. Some people call these Bible study groups or small groups or life groups; whatever the name, they were small gatherings of ten to twenty people where you talk about all things Jesus and life.

It sounded pretty good to me, and I signed up right away because, remember, I was all in. We were told that for the first semester of our group, we would meet weekly on Tuesdays and discuss Mark Batterson's book *The Circle Maker*. Buying the book was easy. Reading the first chapter, per our assignment, was not quite as easy but more painless than I expected. (As you know, I'm not a big reader, but this book was engaging and gave me a new perspective on praying.)

Then, suddenly, the day arrived. It was time to actually show up. To get in the car and drive to the inaugural meeting of my new community group.

Now, I don't know if you've ever been invited to a gathering of women where you don't know any of them (except maybe the host or the one overly friendly neighbor who invited you), but I feel it is always, no matter my age, a little terrifying. In fact, I can work myself up into such a tizzy over not knowing anyone that I will back out of attending things like this entirely. It's a little ridiculous when I say it out loud, but I have done this more than once. Many times more than once.

But this time, whether it was my comfort level with my weight at the time or my hair working particularly well that day, I decided to take a leap and attend the first meeting at Stephanie Payne's home. I had no idea what to expect other than some Jesus conversation, which I was certainly too biblically uneducated to partake in, but I figured I could listen and learn.

When I arrived, Stephanie greeted me at the door with a big

hug and quickly introduced me to several of the women, two of whom I had already met at church. There was food laid out across the kitchen counters and a coffee station. Food and coffee is the right way to start anything, in my opinion. We talked for about twenty minutes and then Stephanie guided us into the living room, where people sat on the sofa, chairs, and the floor. It felt relaxed and comfortable. We talked about that week's chapter of the book, and we shared about our lives, and then we prayed together. Sounds simple, doesn't it? But something beautiful happened in that living room I had never experienced before—a group of mostly strangers became friends.

Let's go back to the "we shared about our lives" part.

We opened up. I mean A LOT. We should have signed waivers that said, "What happens in small group stays in small group." Stephanie had asked each of us, one by one, what she could specifically pray circles around. The first couple of answers were sweet and maybe what I would call polite "surface answers," like someone's daughter had a big exam the next day and someone else's husband had an important business trip coming up. But then the third woman, as soon as Stephanie put a hand on her shoulder, broke down in tears. This sweet woman began to share about her difficulties at home and her husband's addiction to alcohol. She shared her embarrassment and frustration and fear.

Her vulnerability cut right through me. What she shared that day, that painful struggle of an alcoholic spouse, was the very same struggle I was experiencing in my own home. This was a few years before Craig's sobriety and it was something I had been silent about, a deeply buried secret I was too ashamed to share with anyone.

But in my new friend's heartbreaking and raw vulnerability,

she gave me permission to share my own story. Although it took me a few weeks before I felt comfortable enough to speak up, when I did, it was as if the Hoover Dam itself had crashed down in tiny pieces, carrying with it the weight of my shame over Craig's drinking. In that experience, I realized that it took another woman's vulnerability for me to be open and vulnerable about my own struggles. I felt like I had discovered a secret of the universe.

So let's talk about that secret. Vulnerability.

First, being vulnerable is not weak. It can show weakness, but it is in no way weak. Quite the contrary—it takes a lot of courage to share pieces of ourselves with others, especially those areas we perceive as shameful or damaged.

Vulnerability is essential to real connection with other women. If we can agree that the opposite of being vulnerable is being *protected*, then let's imagine that whatever armor is protecting us is also forming a heavy glass barrier between us and those around us. You and others can see each other just fine, and most people won't even realize the barrier is there—until they get close, and *BOOM*. They bump up against your glass. Where we keep the armor, we have the barrier; where we smash it down, we get connection.

The great Brené Brown talks a lot about vulnerability, and I enthusiastically endorse just about everything she says, but I would like to put forth a slightly radical take on one of her pearls of wisdom. "Vulnerability," she says, "is about sharing our feelings and our experiences with people who have earned the right to hear them."[7]

I say maybe we shouldn't always wait until someone has earned the right to hear our experiences. I say we get vulnerable more liberally, sharing some of the ugly stuff when it feels right, even if it's the first or second time we've met. If that woman from my community group at Stephanie's house hadn't shared about her alcoholic husband the first time we met, who knows what precedent would have been set? Who knows how long it would have taken for her words to move me to get vulnerable, what chain of events would have failed to be set off? However, I also very much want to acknowledge that you've got to use some discretion here. There is an appropriate and an inappropriate time to share. If we share too much too fast in certain situations—like when you're on a first date, or at the office, or checking out at the grocery store—it can not only push the other person away but might totally freak them out. And there's no way to guarantee, even in the most appropriate circumstances, that the other person will respond in the way you hope they would.

But if your heart feels compelled to, give it a try. For me, when the day came that I finally told my new community group about the private, shame-inducing struggles in my home and marriage, I surrendered carrying the weight of that secret. I surrendered it to those women and I surrendered it to God. I was instantly lighter, and it was easier. Was my whole life healed at that moment? Of course not. Saying it aloud did not end Craig's addiction or my pain, but I was a little stronger, a little more capable of bearing the weight. I experienced the relief and hope that came with their heartfelt, beautiful, supportive, encouraging hugs and words. I saw empathy in their tears and knew I was not alone. With time, God did heal Craig's addiction and our marriage, but for me, healing started in a room with real, raw, unapologetic sharing between women.

What's wild to me is that every single woman there had something just as raw to share. You would never know it if you passed this group on the street or saw any of us going about our separate daily lives. We were business owners, realtors, photographers, and moms who stayed home to raise their kids. But everyone had something to be vulnerable about. As the weeks passed, our connection to one another became deeper and our hearts and hurts became lighter. By the end of thirteen weeks, we were better women, and we had forged deep, beautiful relationships with one another. We listened each week, supported each other, and prayed for each other. It was unlike anything I had experienced. Together we broke down walls, we felt seen and heard, and more than that, we felt more loved by each other and by God. I saw His love through them.

Stephanie understood that women don't just need one another for coffee dates and carpooling. We desperately need to connect, and that connection happens when we break down and take off the masks and quit saying all the things we think we are "supposed" to say. We just do it; we get down and dirty, we get real.

Now, I'd like to tell you that at the end of that group I started leading my own group and changed many lives, and that those lives went on to change the world, but I didn't. In fact, we left Momentum, the church sweet Stephanie had planted. In those days, I was desperately trying to get Craig to attend church. It was a continual battle on Sundays. He preferred a more conservative service, so we finally settled on one that was a good fit for both of us. "A little bit country and a little bit rock 'n' roll," you might say: Echo Life Church. Pastor Joe spoke to both of our hearts, and Echo is still our church home today. (For the record, I still adore Stephanie and Tim and am so happy to see how Momentum Church has continued to grow and thrive.)

After a few months of Craig and me attending Echo Life,

they opened up registration for those interested in leading a community/life group. My initial thought was "good for them," but there was another thought I could not get out of my head. What I haven't told you is that while I was busy discovering the almost-supernatural power of vulnerability among women, Stephanie was busy trying to talk me into leading a future life group. Me, the girl who did not know the Bible from cover to cover, or heck, even cover to Deuteronomy. She encouraged me to gather women, get to know their hearts, and talk about Jesus. Whatever that might look like, she would say to me, just do it.

Within a few days of seeing Echo Life's call to register, I began to feel such a pull to lead, but pushing back were all the reasons I could not do this. What if someone asked me deep questions like "What happened after the twelve tribes entered Canaan, the Promised Land, for it to become Lebanon, Syria, Jordan, and Israel?" (If you know, shoot me a message.) Or "What book comes after Deuteronomy?" (I'll figure that one out on my own.) What if they needed me to fully understand the Bible and expected me to quote just the right verse at just the right time? I was seriously lacking in biblical education and highly underqualified to lead any group attached to a church.

But then I started to reminisce about that first group of women. My fond memories were not about perfectly quoted biblical knowledge; they were about the way the group made me feel. I felt loved and safe and heard in a time that was otherwise lonely and alienating.

So I took the leap and, despite my fears of not being able to sing the books of the Bible in order to a nursery rhyme, stepped up to lead a group. I have a little spoiler alert for you: it was phenomenal. Like, better than I could have ever imagined in my wildest dreams!

Our group. Let me tell you about this group. It was as though God picked fifteen women who were perfectly made to be a part of something special. We had a range of ages from twenty-five to sixty-five. Some were new in their faith and some had deep biblical knowledge—like Julia, whom we called "the Bible whisperer," because no matter what we were discussing, she would immediately flip to the right page and read a perfect piece of Scripture that sounded written for that exact moment. It was also a fertile collection of women, as three of them conceived while in that group. I am happy to share that I was not one of them.

But what made it one of the most glorious, beautiful groups of women ever brought together was our willingness to be vulnerable with one another. On day one, I pulled a Stephanie and asked each woman how we could pray for her. The women could have kept their answers on the lighter side—mother-in-law visits and kids with sore throats and projects at work—and that would have been fine. Nothing is too small for prayer, and I wouldn't expect everyone to bare their souls the first day anyway. But these women chose, either on that first day or soon after, to get vulnerable. To share the hard stuff. To trust this was a safe place and reveal the things they had kept hidden from the world. Their vulnerability was like a hammer to that wall of glass armor, and as they shared their hurts and shed their tears, every bit of those walls came crashing down.

In some cases, the connection we experience with other women may last for only a season. While everyone in a group will love and treasure each other forever, the season ends, and our schedules and locations mean our paths don't necessarily cross often. But in many cases, a group like this results in precious friendships that don't miss a beat when the original cause for connections wraps up.

One of the women who attended that group was named Melissa Shoemaker. She, her husband, Kylle (yes, two l's), and their baby girl, Kezie, had recently moved to Pensacola. Melissa was immediately engaging and funny, but she came heavy and brokenhearted. Less than a year before she'd lost her brother, Alex, to a tragic boating accident. I immediately connected with her through this since I had lost my sister Kim to cancer the year before. We deeply bonded through our mutual tragedies.

Even though she's fourteen years my junior, our connection felt like it had been there for an eternity, and the more we shared, the more vulnerable we got, and the closer we became. After that first group ended, we began to lead other groups together. Turns out all that theological training I was missing she had in her back pocket (like, with a legit degree)—and now she works full time helping me organize women's retreats.

You can probably guess that with both Melissa and me involved, our retreats rely HUGELY on vulnerability. These ladies have hardly put their purses in the purse corner when I bust out the deep questions. If we're going to have a life-changing weekend, we have to get rid of those barriers real quick. If we want real connection with each other and with God, we gotta get vulnerable.

You see, we are literally better humans when we gather and share authentically and vulnerably with one another. Yet for some reason, we often believe we're the only ones experiencing our current hurts and pains and stresses. Be it the difficulties of raising children, challenges with spouses, loss of loved ones, flailing after children leave, feelings of loneliness, changes in careers, struggles with addictions—we feel what we feel and we assume everyone else is doing just fine.

But guess what? It's not just you. If it were just you, I probably wouldn't be writing this chapter. I'd be taking just you for a coffee. Even if we arrive at the logical conclusion that, yes, we all are bearing emotional burdens every day, how often do we talk to each other about it? When we fail to be vulnerable with one another, we fail to share those loads and to reap the immeasurable benefits of true, deep connection with one another.

I know this because I know what it's like to feel alone and hurt and to not share it. To be too proud or embarrassed to get vulnerable. When Makenzie was a teenager, I was raising her on my own and it was so, so hard. I'd had this sweet little girl with bouncing blonde curls who adored me and called me mommy, and the next thing I knew she was fourteen, slamming doors and telling me she hated me. I felt hurt, devastated, and very alone.

Because I'd had Makenzie at such a young age, none of my friends had teenagers. The fellow moms at school were older, and I felt certain they viewed me as a young dumb blonde and wanted nothing to do with me. (To be honest, even now looking back, I'm not so sure I was wrong. The looks they gave me weren't exactly welcoming.) I wasn't involved in any community groups or mom groups or even attending a church at the time. I was certain that I was just a really bad mom—that I'd done everything wrong, I'd completely ruined my child, and all of her bad behaviors were because of me—and there was nobody to tell me any differently.

One day I was with a friend and one of her friends, having lunch. The new friend happened to have a teenage daughter as well, and she casually mentioned how difficult her daughter was being and that this was "such a hard time." My eyes widened and my heart skipped a beat. I wanted to throw my arms around her and say, "YES, YES, YES! I hear you, I get you, I am there with you!" It felt freeing to talk to her that day and realize I had not single-handedly destroyed my daughter.

From that day forward, every chance I got to talk with other moms of teenagers, I jumped in. I wanted to understand if their children were equally mean. Did they slam doors? Did they have massive mood swings where they were sweet and kind one moment, and the next moment their head turned around three times and they hissed at you like the demon-possessed girl in *The Exorcist*? Was this normal? I was desperate for connection with other moms and needed to know I wasn't alone.

I never really did find women to connect with about the pains of teenagerdom. I got snippets about other unhinged teenagers and I shared snippets about my own, but these conversations were more about comparing notes and laughing it off than actually opening up about how we really felt. Remember, this was before the explosion of mom blogs, before Glennon Doyle published her breakthrough "Don't Carpe Diem"[8] piece, before you could google "does anyone feel as desperate as me?" and get one hundred articles about how normal mother guilt is.

It was like all the moms of the world were scared they were doing it wrong too, and no one would talk about it for fear that the truth would come out about their child-rearing mistakes. I was no different from them. I have to acknowledge that the lack of connection I experienced may have been partly because I didn't know how to get vulnerable and honest and raw about what I was experiencing. I would have been a better mom and certainly had a great deal more sanity if I had been able to share my heaviness of that season.

And now, twenty-some years later, I find myself in a similar boat for a different reason. For the last couple of decades, mommy bloggers (a term I use with true respect and gratitude) have worked so hard and written so prolifically and honestly; in doing so, they've helped to normalize frank and open discussion among women about the struggles of motherhood.

But we don't yet have the equivalent sea change for us diving into the unknowns of the second half. We don't yet have a massive wave of middle-aged women bloggers and authors and speakers and thought leaders having frank and open discussion about the challenges and fears of this new season of our lives. I mean, we're starting to (you're holding Exhibit A in your hand), but all of us need to be part of this shift.

We have to be willing to be vulnerable with one another. To tell each other the truth, to not just moan about our weird skin things and sore hips as we pour another prosecco, but to talk about what's happening on the inside. What keeps us up at night, what thoughts whir about our minds in our quieter moments.

We're not doing each other any favors by trying to make our lives look perfect to the outside world. It ultimately makes you feel disingenuous, and makes other women feel like they're failing. Now hold on, I am not saying do not live in excellence—absolutely do. Celebrate your wins, enjoy your happiness; you might be the very inspiration another woman needs. What I am saying is, be real about those victories; talk about what it took to get there, be honest about the dark moments when you felt discouraged on your journey, acknowledge those who helped you, and share any lessons you picked up along the way. Nobody—not you, not your daughters, not your peers—benefits from you making it look easy.

We women need to get vulnerable with each other now more than ever. This is why I want to take your hand, sit you down, and say *talk to me*. No, really talk to me. You're probably out of practice because, let's be honest, you haven't had a whole lot of time to talk about yourself for the last few years.

Your last few decades might have felt like walking across an anarchic tennis court, with wild balls coming at you from every direction—balls you had to catch and feed or love or file with a report by 5 p.m. or . . . okay, the analogy isn't perfect. But you've been busy. And maybe the people in your life haven't exactly been asking about you either.

So let's get better at letting it all out and calling on other women to do the same. Let's ask each other real questions and give each other real answers. Let's get vulnerable with our peers, with the women who have gone before us, and the young women behind us—women in Bible study groups, in neighborhoods, at work, or in all kinds of unexpected places. We've been through so much at this point in our lives. Let's not hide it.

Eleven

Get a Girl Gang

Community and Raising Each Other Up

*D*o you ever read books and wonder where the authors were when they wrote that book? Like, did this author go on sabbatical to Nantucket and hole up in a cottage with weathered gray shingles and flat-board white trim, and write from sunrise to sunset in a worn, leather-bound notebook? Or did that author spend years upon years jotting down middle-of-the-night epiphanies on a stack of sticky notes that sat on the edge of his bedside table? I think about this deeply during the two or three times a year I actually read books (remember, I'm not a reader). Perhaps because I write books, I also wonder if the writing flows seamlessly for other authors or if they bang their heads against the walls, begging the words to come, as I do. And are the walls any softer in a salty, sea-kissed Nantucket cottage?

Well, if you too have wondered such things, I'm happy to inform you that today is your lucky day. The place where I write my books, plan my retreats, and do all of my creative businessy things is . . . wait for it . . . outside on my porch! Sorry, that was a lot of buildup for a not-so-exciting answer. I work on my porch about eight months out of the year. For the remaining four months—three of which are blazing hot with vicious bloodthirsty bugs, and one is freezing (that's Florida-freezing, which translates to about fifty degrees)—I work inside, in my bedroom. I sit in a big floral-pattern chair that has a matching ottoman I use mostly as a little coffee table, perfectly positioned to look outside through a large double window. My view from that chair includes lush green grass, one large magnolia tree that's currently in bloom, some yellow lilies, hydrangea bushes that are not currently in bloom, and, behind it all, my mom and dad's house. It's a happy view.

But the porch, front or back, is generally my office of choice. Other than the sounds of nature and the occasional sudden barking from my four-legged staff members, Skye and Birdie, my office is quiet, and my view is sublime. The exception to this is when Craig is home. Whenever I am working outside on that quiet porch (and ONLY when I am), he will make his way around the property using one of the very loud things. Whether it's the leaf blower, the lawn mower, the tractor, or anything else that has a high decibel count, he is strangely drawn to that which will take me out of any form of concentration. It is his gift.

Fortunately, last week, my world was quiet and peaceful, and I was writing this book in my swivel rocker on the back porch. I knew I wanted to write about the idea of community but was struggling with how to start it. And God, 'cause He's cool like this, gave me the most wonderful nudge: a phone call from my friend Bridget.

My friend Bridget is elegant, beautiful, brilliant, and driven and has a vibrant, inviting, and infectious personality. She's what I call the whole package. Our friendship has spanned over almost fifteen years, and we have been through a lot of life together. We originally met at a company event for top achievers in Charlotte, North Carolina. Just to be clear, we were the top achievers (*she writes with a not-so-humble grin*). But my initial interaction with Bridget was not so elegant and inviting, because within the space of our first conversation, she explained to me that she did not like or trust female friendships. She told me she would simply rather not have them.

As soon as I heard that, my brows went up and a giant smile crawled across my face. *Ohhhh realllyyy*, I thought with a Jim Carrey, pet detective sort of voice playing in my head. This kind of felt like when you find out a boy isn't interested in you. All of a sudden, he becomes far more appealing. Obviously, her comment was an irresistible challenge to me: I was going to make her my friend till the day she died. And then she was going to go up to Jesus Himself to thank Him for the blessing of our profoundly beautiful and impactful friendship.

I pursued the heck out of that friendship. Over the ensuing three to four years, I was the annoying girl who always hovered around her at events, who just so happened to have the seat next to her at dinners, and who somehow always needed a pee break at the same time as her. I was always so very excited to see her . . . and I showed it. Whether she liked it or not, I was not going anywhere—we were going to be friends. Admittedly part of this was the fun challenge of it all, but I also wanted to show her that female friendships can be wildly wonderful. I guess it worked, or she got tired of resisting me, because today she is one of my closest friends.

Fact check: When I retell Bridget this story about when we met, she completely denies it and claims she never said this. She's wrong. I mean, I think she is. Maybe she actually said she didn't trust salsa and chips. Regardless, who wants to let the truth get in the way of a good story?

But this phone call with Bridget wasn't about catching up on our lives or hairstyles or any of our usual laughs. On this day she was frustrated. Bridget is a top producer in her company and she wanted to take steps to expand her brand through speaking, teaching, and potentially writing a book but was struggling on how to do it. We started talking about email programs, social media, networking opportunities, and so much more. We talked about how she could share her message through churches and her local community. We talked for two hours with ideas flying right and left and could have gone on for another ten. Then as we were winding down our conversation, she said, "Why is all of this so hard to find out about? Why don't we talk about it more?"

Those are very good questions. Her words instantly brought me back to the months after I left my corporate job and transitioned into this new "author-world." I haven't forgotten the agonizing frustration of knowing nothing. I knew nothing about writing, about how to build a brand, an audience, an email list, or navigate through the ever-changing world of social media. And when it came to the actual book process, I knew even less—was I supposed to pursue big publishing houses or self-publish? Did I really need a literary agent? How would I find one, and were there different kinds? Did they handle all genres or did they specialize?

I had a million questions swirling in my mind day after day, and no one I knew seemed to have the answers. I don't think I have ever felt more alone and discouraged than I did during that time.

I broke down in tears a lot in those months after leaving Mary Kay, and I made a promise to myself: I would sincerely try to help the women stepping into this journey behind me. I was angry and disappointed at the world for not delivering answers and solutions to me when I needed them most. I was even frustrated with God for calling me to step out and take a giant leap of faith that was completely devoid of instructions or spreadsheets.

But the truth is, every piece of it is always part of God's plan, isn't it? Something rather beautiful came out of that time. My disheartenment birthed a beautiful idea and started what is often referred to as a "mastermind group."

Now, this wasn't one of those mastermind groups people pay thousands of dollars to be a part of, because honestly, I didn't feel that I had much to offer in that season. Instead, this was a group conceived by a frustrated novice author while sitting alone on her back porch, formed out of desperation and loneliness in hopes that if I (virtually) gathered a few women, collectively we would be able to help each other.

I knew several women who also had taken leaps of faith and were stepping into something new, but they did not know each other. Each had fascinating backgrounds and knowledge about so many things, from banking to photography, but their previous expertise did not seamlessly transfer to their new endeavors. The more I thought about it, the more women came to mind. We were all struggling and feeling a little stuck, and I figured, what the heck—let's all get together and see what we can make happen.

There were originally seven of us: my sister Jodie, who was an incredible artist trying to turn her gift into a business; Jessica, who had left a long career in banking to begin an embroidery business; Sarah, who had a successful established business, Tippi Toes, but had just written her first book and was getting into public speaking; Heather and Amy, who were business coaches; Ashley, who was a successful photographer launching a new nonprofit business; and me. Seven women looking to expand their business and grow, each of us looking for guidance and support in a one-hour Thursday morning Zoom. And you know what? It worked.

Our Zoom calls always began with a little visiting and giggling before launching into that day's topic. Each call's leader was chosen the previous week; we did this by sharing particular challenges we were experiencing, and then the woman with the most experience in that "missing area" would volunteer to lead and teach during the next Zoom. It was perfection. We seven women shared our struggles and challenges with where we were, and then the group offered feedback and solutions. Some had taken online courses, some had attended seminars, and others just had lots of life experience—but when you brought all that knowledge together collectively, it was magnificent! As individuals we were struggling, but as a group we became powerful. We knocked down barriers—like demystifying the various platforms we could use for marketing and quelling one another's doubts that our products and ideas were any good—but I think half the battle was just having someone cheer us on and say we weren't crazy. In hindsight, I can see that I did need answers to some business problems, but more than that, I needed my own personal hype girls . . . and they became that for me. We became each other's hype team.

We were, in a word, a community.

Keep in mind that community can be a fluid concept. My mastermind group lasted about half a year before a range of reasons led us to lovingly disband. Right now, I find community in my own life group through church and the women's groups we created from our retreats. Next year, I might seek and find community somewhere else.

Being an author can be lonely, Nantucket cottages or not. So can being an entrepreneur attempting to bring a wild idea to life. Or a new runner trying to train for a half-marathon. Or a middle-aged daughter who's the sole caretaker of her parents. Heck, being a mother of ten children in a loud, chaotic house where she never has a moment to herself can be lonely. If we are to have the confidence and drive to prioritize ourselves and pursue our personal goals, we need to have a community of women who believe in us and encourage us to believe in ourselves. Listen—I know the whole "when the going gets tough, the tough get going" thing, but that's easier said than done. With community, when the going gets tough, we've got our sisters to help push and pull and shove us through.

There's a story in the Old Testament of when the Israelites were holding off the Amalekite armies. God told Moses that as long as Moses could hold his staff up over his head, Joshua and the rest of the Israelites would have the advantage. But Moses wasn't young and he was getting tired. He'd been holding that staff up a long time. Unfortunately, whenever he started to drop his hands, the Amalekites gained the advantage. As time passed, Moses' arms became so tired that he could no longer keep them raised.

That's when his people stepped in. Aaron and Hur found a stone for him to sit on, then they stood on each side of Moses, holding up his hands for him. Moses was able to persevere, to maintain that vital position until sunset, and as a result, Joshua overwhelmed the army of Amalek in battle (Exodus 17:11–13).

How beautiful is that? There is so much power in a few people (maybe even just two) holding you up when you're too tired to do it yourself, when that goal you've set seems to be creeping further away and your determination to pursue it is dwindling with each passing day.

This is what community is; it's a body of people. And when done right, it's an extension of your own body, your own dreams, your own failures and successes. It's your people who are there to help you and support you during the battles of life and to celebrate in the sweetness of it.

It's not uncommon at this stage of life to find that we know a lot of women, but we're not necessarily in mutually supportive community with those women. We have a college bestie who lives in another state whom we catch up with when we can; we've got the neighbors we chat with outside when the weather's nice; there's the colleague who always makes us laugh; the girls from the book club; the walking partner; and the ladies who love to get together for tapas every few months.

Those relationships can have all types of value, however deep or surface-level your time together is. But community isn't just about finding a nice group on a Wednesday night at Sally's house, is it? The community I'm talking about, the community we need at this pivotal time of life, involves meaningful connection. It can happen in even a very small group (look what Moses managed to do with the support of just two other dudes).

This means articulating what *you need* out of your community and understanding *each other's needs*. In my mastermind group, each woman had clearly stated goals, which helped to illuminate what gifts and wisdom the others should share. For example, if Woman #1 didn't tell us she was embarrassed she'd never learned Excel, then Woman #2 couldn't say, "Girl, I'm great at it; I'm coming Thursday morning with coffee to teach you the basics." And if Woman #3 hadn't admitted she felt paralyzed by impostor syndrome, then Women #4, #5, and #6 might not have tearily said they felt the same and Woman #7 might not have swooped in with techniques to overcome it.

Obviously that was a career-centered group, but the same applies to any area in which you have goals or passions, be they related to career, health, spirituality, cooking, writing, singing, or square dancing. This book is about bringing purpose to your second half; it's about reconnecting with who you are and what you want, and then actively pursuing that. Community is a key part of this journey; we must surround ourselves with support systems and accountability partners.

This might mean taking things up a notch with women who are already in your life, or it might mean reaching outside your current circles and finding new women who seem to either share or complement your interests or ambitions.

It's hard for me to tell anyone how to find a new circle of friends or a healthy group to begin making connections with, so I took some time to consider what I would do if I moved to a new city tomorrow. I would first introduce myself to my neighbors—I don't think we do this enough—then I would pick a church that looked like my style (which is so much easier to research today with online resources). Those are things you can do right now, wherever you are.

Also, have a closer look at the women already in your life. Who has mentioned, perhaps just in passing, something that caught your attention? Something that made you think, *Oh, she thinks about that too?*

I have a friend—we'll call her Mary (her name is not really Mary, it's Shari, and she's my brilliant editor who also has become a dear friend, but she wrote Mary when she edited this, so we'll play along)—who moved to a new country and knew nobody and decided she wanted to start working on a novel. "Mary" got off to a galloping start, but after a few months found that without her beloved writing group from her previous town, she was lacking motivation and finding excuses to do anything but write. (Can I relate to that? Nah, of course not. Why would you say that?)

Her dream was getting blurrier and blurrier, and then one morning, it hit her: If she kept at this alone, the novel wasn't going to happen. She remembered a conversation from months earlier, when an acquaintance had made a comment about a woman in the neighboring town who was also a writer. Mary Facebook-stalked the woman until she found a way to contact her, then sent this simple message: *"I know this is weird and you don't know me, but I'm trying to write a book and I'm feeling stuck. I heard you write too. Do you want to meet for coffee and talk about writing?"*

Guess what? The other woman acted like it wasn't weird at all, the two met and talked, and to this day they still have a weekly standing writing date. They set deadlines for each other, they exchange and critique each other's work, they discuss their challenges and brainstorm ideas, and they lift each other up when the ideas don't come.

Look around you. Who can you send a weird unsolicited message to? If your first attempt isn't a perfect fit, keep trying until you meet your people.

When I listen to Craig recommend AA meetings to those

struggling with drinking, he always adds the caveat, "You may not find the right fit immediately, but keep going to different groups until you find a group that feels more like your people." I feel the same way about finding a good group of women. If you go into a group and you think, *These are not my people; they're all a bunch of fruitcakes*, try another one. It's not the end of the world. God made good groups for all of us and we all have a little fruitcake in us, but maybe you need the strawberry ones and instead you went to the blueberry one. If you don't find it, I give you full permission to start your own little group of strawberry fruitcakes. Whatever the case, don't give up on finding your sisterhood. It is out there, I promise you.

We know our people when we meet them, don't we? I'm at an age now where I can feel it in minutes. I know there's something between us and we will just get each other a little more easily. Meeting other women is not much different from dating (if I recall correctly . . . it's been a long time); there are some we connect with right away and some we don't. And there are some we fight for (ahem, Bridget).

Now, maybe you're thinking, *I work with a bunch of women and they're dramatic and crazy and suck the life out of me. There is no way I am going to go seek more women in my life.* Whoa, Nelly. The truth is, you are in an unhealthy environment, and the majority of women do not behave that way. Seeking your community can be intimidating, but remember this: Women as a whole are kind and welcoming. No matter what the world and news tell you, most people are good.

If you're sitting over there and saying to yourself, *That's just for Dawn. Dawn seems like more of a social person and that's probably just her jam*, nope, that's wrong. I have worked with so many women of every personality type, every age, and every season, and I can tell you we need one another. We need each other more than these words will ever be able to express to you. You're not meant to walk through this life alone. You are meant for community and fellowship. It's how we are wired and it's biblical. It's like the secret sauce or South Louisiana's Fezzo's seasoning. Everything is just better with other women.

There is an old African proverb that says, "If you want to go fast, go alone. If you want to go far, go together." We are meant to go far TOGETHER, not alone. There are so many things I do not know about life, but I know this: We are stronger and better together. When you bring together a band of women in the right way, you find community and fellowship. You will be stronger, your load will be lighter, your perspective will change. You will feel less alone. We empower each other to become our best selves. But it rarely happens by chance. You must actively pursue community and foster it. Gather your fellow masterminds. Find your "Erin and Her" (if you'll indulge me in a little Moses wordplay). Get yourself a girl gang.

twelve

Wow! You're Still Here

Redefine Relationships in the Second Half

If we look at our list of friends and see that it's shorter and more robust than ever, I believe we've done something right. We've accepted that we have those we talk to daily and ones we speak to every six months, and the bond with all of them can be equally profound. With marriage, it's harder to tell if we've "done it right." I have married friends trying to decide whether to double down or jump ship. I have some single friends who struggle with having never married and other single friends who find the appeal of tethering to a partner for life completely baffling. Half my divorced friends look exhausted from the new norms they're adjusting to while the other half has never looked healthier and happier.

What we all have in common is that now, as we're entering

the second half of our lives, relationships don't look the way they did when we were younger. Relationships—like the people in them—change over time. The definition of a good friendship or a good marriage is slippery and subjective, and some trait you gave no thought to when that relationship first formed might be the very thing keeping you connected now. So how do we make sure our relationships continuously evolve to be deeper and sweeter than we ever imagined?

For me, the place I've explored this question most is within my own marriage, so I'm going to start with that.

I'm not gonna lie, I bet there are a few people out there who lost a decent amount of money on the bet of whether Craig and Dawn would still be married after one year, many of whom were my own family members. Heck, *I'm* even shocked that we're still married sometimes, especially when I look over and see that he has yet again chosen to go in public with an outfit that looks like it was given to him by a homeless man because he, the homeless man, felt sorry for Craig. In Craig's defense, I'm also shocked that he is still married to *me* when I do stupid things like . . . well, oddly, none are coming to mind right now, but I'm sure there's something. (There are benefits to being the author.)

We are two people who are opposite in just about every way imaginable except our faith, humor, politics, and moral guidelines. I guess those are pretty big, but there's also the fact that he is always late, he never wants to go anywhere (maybe because he flies planes for a living), and he leaves everything, everywhere, every day.

If you think about it, the whole thing really is odd. Two people in their midtwenties consider each other to be so appealing that they want each other to be the first thing they see EVERY DAY

FOR THE REST OF THEIR LIVES. The plan is that they will not just get along, but love each other and want to be intimate with each other over and over and over for like, forty-eleven years. They will raise animals and humans together and, again, be intimate over and over and over. It's a lot to ask. In fact, it was so much to ask of me, I needed another shot at it. This is my second marriage and, if I have anything to say about it, my last one.

Craig and I have been married for nineteen years. Our marriage started after a quick four-month courtship originating from slightly dishonest match.com posts; he lied about dipping tobacco and I looked, well, a little larger in person. But we fell in love fast and, as my grandmother used to say, "It stuck."

Craig and I don't have a fairytale story; our road has been challenging, hard, and even tragic at times. We went through things together in our first ten years of marriage that most don't experience in a lifetime. Craig's battle with alcoholism—he's more than eight years sober now—my breast cancer, the loss of family members, and so much more.

We had years where Craig was using alcohol to numb every feeling and I was spending our money like a drunken sailor in the port of Thailand who'd just spent nine months at sea. We were two hurt and angry people.

We could go from playing the silent game to bursting into screaming matches like it was a party trick. And we had this weekly dance of sorts every time work took him out of town for a few days. On day one of his return, he'd come home and all would be well for a day. Day two he would get drunk and we'd fight, then day three he'd be remorseful and then leave again. Same dance, almost every week, for a very long time. We tried to behave like a normal and happy family, especially for the sake of our daughter,

Ella, but it's impossible to hide that much pain and hurt from a child, even when you think you are.

I remembered there being a time when things were so bad that I actually prayed for our marriage to end. I didn't believe God could heal something so damaged. But sometimes God's answer to prayer is no, and our marriage didn't end.

I can't pinpoint what year or what season it was, and nothing happened overnight, but God did heal our broken marriage. I don't know if I was just too worn out, or because my fear of being single and having to buy new bras was greater than my desire to win a ridiculous argument about the lights being left on, but somewhere in it all, we shifted for the better. Craig sought help for his drinking and I put a lid on the spending—except when it came to throw pillows, because I'm not a Tibetan monk and throw pillows make all homes a little warmer.

We began talking more—a lot more. We made more eye contact. We started to make more effort to be kind to each other, and we responded with gratitude and even joy. Screaming matches became a thing of the past, and authentically listening became an actual thing (go figure). Somehow we became more "on purpose" about our marriage than ever before, and it morphed into two middle-aged people who not only loved each other but actually liked each other; we became partners, lovers, and friends.

Today I love this homeless-dressing man so deeply that the very thought of walking this road of life without him brings tears to my eyes. He is my perfect partner and will forever be my soft place to fall. I know I'm better with Craig Barton by my side.

This place we have come to, this sweet season, is beautiful. It feels a little like a washing of peace has covered our marriage.

There's an easiness and confidence that wasn't there in the early years.

This smoother season of ours, although sometimes laden with bickering, has been one of the first times we fully have "had each other's back." A little sad to say after almost twenty years of marriage, isn't it? We now understand the big picture collectively and are moving together rather than as two individual people seeking our own goals. Do we still have individual goals? Absolutely, but they are pieces of our bigger picture *together*.

I think marriage feels almost easy for us today because it was so hard for us for so many years. We used to battle over our roles and who worked harder or who did more or who was more worn out, like there was some trophy to win if one of us put in more hours than the other. Now there is an appreciation for what the other does, and we take the time to acknowledge it. Two days ago he stopped in the middle of a walk and said, "I just want to thank you for what you do for my mom. There aren't a lot of wives who would let their mother-in-law live with them, and you embrace it so beautifully." I'll be honest, I was blown away; he's sort of a man of few words. That simple act would not have happened in the bad years. It's proof we're in a vastly different place. Now we do little things like kiss each other good morning and good night for no other reason than we actually like each other.

Do we still argue? All the time! We're one of those snarky kind of couples, and we like going back and forth. But this is our groove; this is what works for us. He makes me laugh more than anyone, and he gets me—I mean *really, really gets me*—more than any person ever has. Does this mean he recently thought it was a good idea to buy me a sinus nasal cleansing machine FOR MY BIRTHDAY? Yes, yes it does. Our marriage is a work in progress.

But for the most part, there's something beautiful that happened in our marriage that only the passing of time and the wisdom gained from hardships could have done, and it's wonderful.

I know the story of my marriage isn't for everyone, but I share it because it might speak to someone. The whole premise of this book is that we're at this huge pivot point in our lives, and we must embrace this moment and all the opportunities and wisdom and hope that come with it. But we also have to acknowledge that this is a time of great uncertainty and transition.

During big changes and pivot points in life—like a change of careers, children coming along, children leaving for college, retirement, or whatever it may be—we often experience a lack of clarity in our purpose. When we feel like we don't know who we are anymore and question our place in this new world, it rocks us to the core. There can be an overwhelming desire to shed whatever isn't "working." Among the married women in my life, I know many have hit a sweet stride in their marriage while so many others are taking a hard look at their marriages and deciding they don't like what they see.

If that latter is you, I'm in no position to advise you on whether to fight for your marriage. There is certainly more than one woman reading this who has long been in a destructive or abusive relationship; she's been counting the seconds until the last kid takes off for college so she can finally pack her bags and leave without feeling guilty. For you, I pray for the safety and peace you deserve.

But maybe your discontent is the result of years of neglecting your relationship or taking it for granted, of viewing your spouse as nothing more than a partner (or worse, an adversary) with whom you had to coordinate running a household and raising kids. If that's your situation, try to see this pivot point as an opportunity to reclaim the enthusiasm that first made you enter into this crazy commitment. Enjoy the process of discovering what marriage in the second half can look like.

Interestingly (*or so she thinks*), much of what I've just said can also apply to our long-term friendships.

Some of them form when we're young and hot and always up for a good time, then they hit the rocky years when our separate lives make it hard to nurture what's there. Now we find ourselves at this glorious midpoint, taking stock of which friendships survived the storm and reassessing what and who matters.

In my younger years, before husbands and children, my closest friends seemed to be more about who was available to go out on a Friday night, had a little extra cash, and was a really good dancer. But having my first daughter at the age of nineteen then experiencing wave after wave of trauma within three years threw me into a kind of friendless zone. I was so much younger than the other moms and I was the single one, so I felt like I didn't fit in at their playdates and coffee mornings. I was mentally and physically spent, trying to piece back together my shattered life and figure out my path as a woman, a professional, a mother, a functioning human.

So it wasn't until I was in my early thirties that I started to remember what a treasure true friendship was. I began to reconnect with my oldest friends and sought quality newer friendships. Then, as I entered into my forties, God seemed to hand me a silver plate with the most precious friendships through Mary Kay. In fact, they were so precious that they are still my closest friends as I write this book.

While I have fewer friends than I used to, my friendships are deeper than they are wide. I suppose I've never done well with frivolous friendships. Like my friend Melissa says about mommy playdates, if you can't go deep with me fast, then we're not doing it again. I feel this. I have reached an age that if you cannot be real, authentic, and vulnerable with me, we probably won't be friends. Friendships take work and effort.

My friendships now are tight, and I'm a fierce protector of my sisters. I take time to make sure these relationships are healthy, and that these women know they are loved by me. My friendships are not the kind where we need or want to talk to each other every day—sometimes we don't even talk every month—but our love is solid. These women stretch me in my faith, in my work, as a mother, and as a wife. They make me better.

Through the years I have figured out that one friend (or spouse) does not have to serve all my needs. I mean, that's a lot to put on one human. My closest friends—Kali, Casie, Wendy, Bridget, Charlotte, Caroline, Tammy, and Melissa (y'all know they will jump all over me if I don't put their names in here)—each have different giftings, and I love that. I adore them fully but tend to turn to different ones for different things. One friend is a brilliant strategist, and when I want to talk business or explore psychological thoughts, I turn to her. Another is incredibly loving and the kind of human who always makes you feel like you're the most wonderful person on the planet. Another is the one I simply do the most "life" with; our children are the same ages and our lives are similar. Another friend gives me wise spiritual counsel. Another always makes me laugh.

Just to be clear, each one of them has ALL of these giftings, but I resonate with some more than others in certain areas.

I love each of these women totally, utterly, and completely, but I also love that they serve different purposes in my life. I don't mean that one is less valuable than another. I am simply saying that God has gifted me with women with the perfect gifts for my needs.

This does not mean friendship is based on serving *our* needs. We should be filling each other's cups. When God presents us with women in our lives who are spent and broken, barely getting through the days and having nothing left to give, we should recognize that God may very well have put us in their lives to fill *their* cups.

It's a lot to expect that one person could be everything to us, be it a spouse or a friend. I suspect that this is why God makes so many beautifully different people with different giftings. What a shame it would be if we only had one deep relationship in our lives.

This is why I think it is so important that, no matter what age we are, we should continue to make friends. Kali's grandmother—Grandma Deedle, the fantastically feisty ninety-nine-year-old I mentioned in chapter 5—still tries to make friends whenever she can. She seeks younger friendships, partly because she wants to stay connected to what's happening in the world outside her high-rise condo, but mostly because she has now outlived all of her own friends. She says her younger friends keep her young.

Did you get that? Even at ninety-nine years old, she actively seeks new friendships and works to cultivate the relationships she has. Kali recently came across her twelve-year-old daughter, Maddy, FaceTiming with Grandma Deedle. Yes, Grandma Deedle is a FaceTimer. She'd contacted Maddy and set *an appointment* for them to visit because, at ninety-nine, she knows unequivocally the value of cultivating relationships.

Curating our friendships doesn't happen by magic. If we are not deliberate about it, we can find ourselves investing in the wrong friendships and neglecting the right ones. By the middle of our lives, we need to have the ability to release friendships and relationships that are not good for us. One of the easiest gauges is, after spending time with that person, do you feel better about yourself or worse about yourself? If you find that someone in your life is consistently making you feel deflated or discouraged, it's time to let that friendship go.

(But before you do, have a quick look in the mirror to take stock of things. Realizing that you cannot change another person and can only be responsible for working and bettering yourself is one of the big aha, slap-you-in-the-face things about life. When we focus on being a better, kinder, and more loving human, the rest of it does get a little easier.)

There are so many people out there who will love you for who you are and breathe belief into you. You do not have to stay in the relationships that don't do this. Friendships are meant to be blessings in your life, cup fillers, soul renewers. I feel that God has handpicked each one of the glorious women in my life, and collectively we do better things for His kingdom because we are a part of each other's lives. I pray that you have these sorts of friendships too. If you don't, I hope that this chapter will gently nudge you toward opening your heart to new friends.

You deserve sweet, precious, and good relationships in your life. Growing is hard, changing is hard, getting older is really hard, but having familiar faces by your side to walk through it with is a beautiful gift.

thirteen

Don't You Dare Call Me Grandma

Redefine What It Looks Like to Be a Grandma in Today's World

*M*om, we're pregnant."

I *want* to tell you that in hearing those words, my heart skipped beats with insurmountable delight. I *want* to describe the tears that poured out of my eyes because the massive amounts of joy I was experiencing could not be held in my body a moment longer. But you and I are way past my telling you big fat lies. The truth is, my initial reaction was more like "Have you lost your ever-lovin' mind?"

I was pretty sure they were too young for babies, but more importantly, I knew *I* was WAY too young to be a grandmother.

Based on my experience, being a grandmother meant being a mawmaw. And there was no way that I—standing there in my ripped capri jeans and fake Gucci belt, setting my gluten-free muffin down on my granite countertop, and only half-listening to my daughter while half-trying to figure out if I was going to be late to my eyelash extension appointment—was ready to step into the orthopedic lace-up shoes of my mawmaw, Norma Thibodeaux Leger.

Norma Leger was the closest thing I've ever known to a real-life saint. Mawmaw was born in the 1920s and raised on a small farm in South Louisiana, Cajun Country. She had four siblings—three brothers and one sister—and her parents spoke only French. To save you googling, here's why: French and Acadian people had settled in Nova Scotia in the mid-1700s, but because people can be mean, they were forced from that area and found their way to Louisiana, bringing with them the language. Most came on ships, which is why there's not a two-thousand-mile trail of French-speaking villages between the Nova Scotia peninsula and Bourbon Street.

Now, by the time Norma became my mawmaw, she spoke English too, because between 1920 and 1960 using the French language was forbidden in virtually all aspects of life in South Louisiana. (Ironically, today "Louisiana French" is taught around the state and in universities.) But when I was a little girl and my mom made me visit my great-grandmother's house, I had to sit in the living room looking out the window at the playground across the street while the adults chatted away in a language I didn't understand. The makings of a miserable visit for a kid.

Of course, in hindsight, I wish I had taken advantage of Mawmaw's role as translator and asked my great-grandma a gazillion questions about her life and who she was. Instead, one of the only things I know is that when my great-grandmother lived back on the farm, she accidentally drove their car through the garage. She refused ever to drive again, and that's why Mawmaw would have to pick her up and take her everywhere. Kind of a brilliant move, if you ask me.

But I think Mawmaw would have chauffeured my great-grandma around town in any scenario because of how kind she was. When my dad speaks of her, he always says, "Norma Leger was the finest human I've ever known"—and she was his mother-in-law, which says a lot.

By the time Mawmaw graduated from high school, World War II had started. (I love this next part of her life story.) Mawmaw boarded a bus with only young women who had never left that part of Louisiana before and they headed for Fort Worth, Texas, to work on airplanes. Yes, airplanes. My grandmother was a machinist who worked on the B24 Liberator. I asked her so many times about this season of her life, but she rarely divulged details. Over the years I picked up little tidbits, like that she lived in a house with all the other women and they loved getting dressed up and going to dances. In fact, she dated and almost married a soldier who was a doctor from New Jersey. But there is so much I'll never know. Anytime she did tell me something about her past, she would smile a little as if keeping a secret she knew she'd never reveal.

Oh, and Mawmaw was a hottie. She was a brunette stunner. I have a photo of her during that time in Texas sitting on a waterfall of stairs, with a long dress fanned out to her side. She looked like a movie star, the old Hollywood goddesses of glam, only she was prettier.

After the war, Mawmaw returned to Louisiana, where she

met and married my grandfather, Luke Leger. Together they raised three children: Darryl, my uncle; Marlene, my mom; and Brenella, my aunt whom I call Nanny.

(Critical side note for you: My grandfather was redheaded, as was my uncle and my mother. I'm asked all the time where Ellason gets her glorious red hair, so now you know. It was not the UPS man.)

When I was born, my parents lived in Lafayette, Louisiana, and Nanny and Mawmaw lived in a much smaller Louisiana town called Rayne, which was about twenty miles away. I was the first-born grandchild in my family, and the world all but stopped that blessed Easter Sunday in March when I entered into it. I was the most beautiful child ever born in the great state of Louisiana and the entire world. I know this to be a fact because my mawmaw told me so, and Norma Thibodeaux Leger never lied.

Every Friday afternoon Nanny and my soon-to-be "uncle" Mike would pick me up and toss me in the back of the car, which, back then, was like two large sofas on wheels and utterly devoid of any safety devices. So it was quite literally like putting a kid in a moving playroom. I stayed with them from Friday afternoon until family lunch on Sunday when my mom would pick me up—again, in a moving playhouse.

My dad was in the oil business and worked offshore, one week home and one week gone, so I suspect those weekends provided a much-needed break for my mom. But life took a wild turn when my dad was transferred overseas with his company, and we spent the next fourteen years of my life in far-off countries like England, Dubai, Singapore, Norway, and Scotland. These places felt like a million miles from my Cajun roots and my mawmaw's beloved house.

Those years of being overseas were a wonderful adventure for me. We moved every two or three years, much like families in the military did. This life brought so many different friends and cultures, and I even learned bits and pieces of other languages (I can still say "milk" in Norwegian). But that period also came with one extra special touchstone: I got to spend every summer and Christmas holiday break back in Rayne. It made the time I had with my mawmaw much sweeter, and even as a child, I treasured it. I think my entire family appreciated our time together because we knew it was limited, and the sands of summer and Christmastime would always run out.

Each year my mom, my sister Kim, and I would fly from overseas into Houston on a massive 747 jet. This was back in the seventies and eighties, when airline travel from overseas was a little like a disco-era cocktail party. People moved about the aisles with a cigarette in one hand and a dirty martini in the other. Children were let loose to visit the stewardesses (that's what they called flight attendants back then), and they'd take us up front to say hello to the pilots. Meanwhile, my mom would make a pallet on the floor at her feet where we spread out our toys and played. Seems like we always had the row of four seats in the middle of the plane. Oh, how the great journey in the friendly skies has changed; I cough a little just from remembering those smoke-filled cabins.

From Houston, we'd transfer to a small puddle-jumper plane for the final leg to Lafayette—the land of love, Mawmaw, Pawpaw, Nanny, Uncle Mike, and gumbo!

Once we returned from the airport, we always made a beeline for Mawmaw's house. We'd go up the three side-porch steps, open the screen door, and enter the mudroom, then grab the crystal glass doorknob that was always a little loose and turn to enter my happiest of all happy places. There'd be a table laid out with our favorite foods. She'd spend days preparing and cooking all of our favorite things—gumbo, potato salad, cold sliced cucumbers dressed with vinegar and salt and pepper. (We had cucumbers at every single meal, and today when we are having family dinner at my house, my own mother will ask where the cucumbers are.) If Mawmaw's gumbo was showing us her love, then her desserts were a glimpse into heaven itself. Fruit salad, chocolate cake with a pineapple filling, and pies—real pies. Coconut pie and chocolate pie and Mawmaw's "refrigerator cookies." I have more childhood memories around her table than any other. Through her food, she expressed exquisite love.

Now that you know all about my mawmaw, fast-forward with me forty years, back to that conversation with my twenty-two-year-old daughter who was trying to tell me I was about to become a grandmother. Me? I couldn't cook. I didn't have a pantry lined with jars of canned figs made fresh with figs from my neighbor's tree like Mawmaw did. I bought my salad in pre-washed bags from Publix and got all my hams already smoked and sliced. And even if I did know how to pick figs from someone's yard and make cans of sweet, spreadable deliciousness, when would I have time to? I was still chasing a three-year-old and trying to earn pink Cadillacs.

Listen, I know all babies are blessings, but I still had one of those sweet blessings running around my house. I guess that's what can happen when you have daughters seventeen years apart: one having a baby while one is still a baby. (Just to be clear, that toddler is sixteen now and still my baby.) The mere thought of

Makenzie having a baby was exhausting. My Ellason was scarcely potty-trained at three and a half, and I was worn out by keeping up with her because I was—and I just love this phrase—"of advanced maternal age." Survival and sleep were at the top of my agenda at that time, and I can assure you grandmotherdom was nowhere on my to-do list.

So you can see where my awful response to the news of my daughter having a baby may have come from. I was not qualified to be a mawmaw. I was far from being the matriarchal gentlewoman that my grandmother was.

Nevertheless, the months passed, Makenzie's belly grew, and the idea of a precious baby girl entering into the family sounded a little sweeter. But I was NOT going to be "Grandma." I announced that the little angel could call me Gigi (short for Glamorous/Glorious Grandmother, you pick). I explained to Makenzie that under no uncertain terms was I going to step into any preconceived ideas the world had of what it meant to be a grandmother. I was a mom to a little one. I had a thriving business and a household and social life to maintain. Plus, during that season, I was doing it all as a single mom because Craig was deployed to Bahrain. I would accept the role of Gigi, this fantastically cool human in the baby's life, but I just could not be "Mawmaw."

And the truth is, my daughter never expected me to be that kind of grandmother. Heck, I wasn't even that kind of mother. Why on earth would I suddenly transform into a gentle granny in a rocking chair?

Kyla Alaine arrived in the spring of 2011, and wouldn't you know it, the world all but stopped that blessed day in April. I felt for her the same inexplicable deep love I had for my own daughters when they were born. Limitless, boundless love. She was perfection, and that child could call me anything—Meemaw, Ma, Granny, Grandma . . . whatever she wanted—just as long as she always called me.

Three weeks after Kyla was born, I was diagnosed with Stage III, triple negative breast cancer, and I soon received my first chemotherapy treatment. A couple of weeks later, Makenzie called to say she was bringing little six-week-old Kyla to visit. I was feeling weak, nauseous, a little scared, and emotionally defeated. Then Makenzie arrived with Kyla, put her in bed with me, and tears fell from my eyes. Oh, the feeling that went through me. I looked at her and thought, *I can't believe that there was ever a moment that I thought you weren't the most perfect idea in the world.*

I stared at her and soaked in the curve of her lips, her eyes, her fuzzy hair. I'd shaved my head two days earlier and we looked a little like twins at that point. I wanted to inhale her sweetness. In that moment, with that tiny human nestled warmly in my arm, I knew that even bald, sick, and weak, I was the perfect grandmother for her. With all my flaws and faults, I was made to be her grandmother. I was Gigi and she was my Ky-Fry.

~

Lying in bed with Kyla, loving her with every ounce of my being even when I didn't have the strength to lift her little twelve-pound body, was when I realized that the magical thing about Mawmaw wasn't that she could create celestial meals. It was the way she made me feel.

Looking back, I realize Mawmaw was incredibly busy. She worked full time as the night receptionist at the local hospital while also running her household and, as I may have mentioned, feeding everybody. She tended to every need of her family and was a generous, attentive friend and neighbor. Despite all of this, she still made me feel like I was the only person in the world who mattered. That everything else could go by the wayside just as long as she had me to love. I saw it in the way she looked at me and in the words she spoke to me; I was magnificently treasured.

So maybe you can understand why I was always so excited to see her. Every summer and Christmas, as our plane's wheels skimmed the surface of the tarmac, I would press my face to the window, desperately searching for silhouettes of my family. I scoured the big glass windows of the terminal so hard until I could see them, and then my excitement would build to such an explosive level that tears would begin to flow at the mere thought of embracing them.

As soon as Mawmaw and Nanny saw the plane touch down, they would begin frantically waving as if flagging down a rescue vessel and shouting, "We're here, we're here!" I could see them while we taxied and parked and waited for God knows what. I remember those moments of waiting so vividly. I have no idea what they do between landing a plane, parking it, and letting people off, but it still to this day feels like the moment you are waiting for the bachelorette to announce who gets the final rose.

One summer, I just wasn't having it, and the excitement overcame me. I dropped the safety of my mother's hand and wormed my way up to the front. At this time, going to the terminal meant disembarking via a rickety set of metal stairs and walking across the tarmac toward the building. I ran down the stairs from the plane and began weaving in and out of the passengers already down there as if I were a race car frantic for the Mawmaw finish line. Once I broke out in front of the group, I ran to be the first to reach the terminal. Honestly, I was moving at full speed. But I missed one detail: the large glass door between myself and my family was still closed. I ran in such a way that my forehead was the first to hit the glass, and then my body followed. It was a huge wall of glass; it made a thud, and I think I even felt it move a little.

Don't worry, I was fine, but the evidence of this incident remained on my forehead for many weeks of my trip in the form of a large red then greenish-black knot. I'm sorry to say that this is not the only time I've walked into a glass door thinking it was open, as I've never been one for grace or patience. But I do think it was my highest-velocity impact.

Mild concussion or not, our reunions were glorious! Mawmaw would grab me, pull me close in a long, tight hug, then push me away to look at me and say, "Cher Bébé!" (which means dear/darling baby). She'd then proceed to repeatedly smack my upper arms so hard she'd actually leave a mark. It was as if she was a shaken-up Coke bottle, and her love was CO_2 pushing to escape. With each one of those pats, a small amount of "fizz" was released to stop the Mawmaw bottle from bursting open. You could see explosive love in her face and definitely feel it every time. And she loved all of us like that, not just the Easter-born Golden Child.

When I was very young, I wanted to be like Mawmaw. I wanted to have a house that always smelled like a blend of Coty loose face powder from her bathroom, vanilla extract from something baking in her kitchen, and fresh laundry from the towels hanging to dry on her clothesline. I wanted a kitchen table covered in colorful, abundant dishes. I wanted to sneakily whisk away my future grandkids' dirty clothes and return them folded and clean on their beds like a laundry fairy. I wanted them to see me the way I saw her: a selfless, kind, joyful, humble woman of God who loved all out, no matter who you were.

But at some point, long before that fateful announcement from Makenzie, I began to realize that I was not going to be Mawmaw 2.0. I had no idea how to—or desire to—even make a roux, the most basic of grandmotherly skills, in my eyes. (After all, how will people know you really love them if you can't show them through gumbo? I can only assume this is why people outside of Louisiana are less happy than people in it—the food.) I accepted that my grandchildren were never going to sit back and reminisce about anything I had ever cooked them. NEVER.

And Mawmaw's faith. Boy. I vividly remember during my stays at her house how every night my grandparents would pray on the sides of their beds, on their knees, on a hard, wood floor. Every single night. In fact, one of the few times I would ever get fussed at was when I tried to interrupt this prayerful time. I knew it was sacred. Now, I love Jesus and I get my prayers in every day, but if I got on my knees to pray, I'm not sure I could ever get up again.

Mawmaw was also an excellent housekeeper; I, on the other hand, can let laundry pile up till I'm down to one last pair of panties and even then get creative with some swimsuit bottoms. Now hush, you know I'm teasing because this body hasn't seen a bikini since the 1980s, and I sure can't get any part of this slightly expanded body into those bottoms even if I did still own them, but you get my point.

When Kyla was about eighteen months old, Makenzie and her husband divorced and she remarried a wonderful man, Landon. Landon was also divorced and had a precious little girl the same age as Kyla named Chloe. She had gorgeous brown hair kissed with caramel highlights from endless days at the beach and these big brown eyes that swallowed my soul the first time I met her. She was one of the most precious and unexpected gifts of my life.

Over the next few years, I got two more grandchildren—Sawyer, with his blinding fuzzy blond hair, and then Sutton, with that identical towhead fuzz. I think they all came out with bronzed skin begging to be soaked in the sun every day. That same overwhelming love I experienced with Kyla flooded through me with these three as well. It was like magic.

Today, Ky-Fry and Chlo-Bug are twelve, Saw is seven, and Sutty is four, and I only feel that overwhelming love even more overwhelmingly—although I have no idea why we can't just call them their real names.

In most ways I'm nothing like the grandmother I once thought I would be. But there's one exception.

I wanted to be the type of grandmother that my grandchildren adored; I wanted them to feel about me the way I felt about my mawmaw. Her love for me was one of the single greatest gifts of my life, and I wanted my grandchildren to one day feel the same.

On that aspect, I'm nailing it. (Or so I think I am. Check the reviews of this book and see what my grandkids say.)

They are big, loud, beautiful blessings in my life. We live about an hour and a half away from each other, so our time tends to be more planned than spur-of-the-moment. But when they are around, my mindset shifts; they may make me feel physically old sometimes, but they certainly make me think younger. When was the last time you picked up a Nerf gun? Let me tell you, I don't care how old you are, playing Nerf gun wars will take you back to childhood in a heartbeat. Sawyer is the best at this right now and he is ALL IN, and Sutton isn't far behind, wanting to mimic everything his big brother does.

And I'll tell you something else—I don't recall my children needing to eat, like, at all. But my grandchildren ask for food every single hour when they're here, from morning to night. They are bottomless pits of vivacious energy. Is it because I keep terribly junky food here that their mom wouldn't let them eat? Maybe. That's a small part of my master plan to brainwash them all to believe Gigi's house is the best place on earth, and hey, it's working.

They say one of the best things about being a grandparent is that you get to give them back when you're tired, and it's true. I love having them all over here, but I sort of don't mind when they leave either because I am guaranteed to be flat-out exhausted. Chasing babies is a young man's game, as my husband says.

Grandparenting has also reminded me that kids cry much easier than grown-ups do. They cry about things like not being able to sleep with that stick they found outside in the mud two hours ago, or that their applesauce touched their macaroni on their plate, or that their sisters are riding on the golf cart without them. (Okay, I get that one—no one wants to be left behind.) Crying is fast, loud, and easy for kids. Maybe it should be more acceptable for adults too; maybe a quick sob now and then would let us release all of our tensions throughout the day and we'd just be happier. Something to think about.

I love being a part of my grandkids' lives. I love being able to shape and guide them, to brainwash them about never wearing white shoes after Labor Day and that the University of Alabama really is a school where bad things happen. Dead bodies are buried under the Denny Chimes tower, monsters roam around Marr's Spring, and no one should ever go there. You can go anywhere else, but never Alabama. (Oh, quit your cryin', Bama fans—get your own darn book and you can complain about LSU in it. This one's mine and I get to say things like this.)

One reason I tell you all this is because there is one way I am a textbook grandparent: I can't stop talking about my grandkids. So you have to hear about them.

The other reason is because I suspect many of you have already found—or are about to find—yourself in this new role, and I want you to know it's okay if you're not instantly ecstatic about it. It's okay if it takes a while to figure out what kind of granny you're going to be, what you want to be called, what your stance is on brownies for breakfast, and other important grandparent questions. Maybe you've barely had time to reckon with your new identity as an empty nester, and now you've got this new hat to wear. But I did it and you can too.

Other than writing an entire chapter about my grandkids, I'm still not the stereotypical grandmother. But I am the perfect grandmother for them, and you will be for yours. That's how God does it. He knows who we are in our mother's womb, and He knows what and who we need in our lives. For me, it was Mawmaw. For my little squirts, well, they've got me.

Fourteen

A Big Juicy Sandwich

Find the Joy in Caring for Children and Parents

*W*hen I was young and fantasized about my future, dreaming about my husband, my 2.5 children, and my amazing antebellum home with a wraparound porch, I never once envisioned my parents being a part of any of it. Granted, I was a little self-centered and very naive, but when I saw myself rising from the distressed oak rocking chair and gliding down those grand entry stairs, Mom and Dad were never standing about twenty feet away engaged in a heated debate over why magnolia trees drop so many leaves. And not once did my fantasy include me heading to the guest house next door to bathe and wipe the heinie of another elderly family member. Nope, not once.

I have no idea why I thought I'd live in a big antebellum home because the truth is, I'm ridiculously scared of old houses. I fear that in all old homes someone has died and is pacing back and forth in their room, gazing out the window longingly, awaiting the return of their true love. And if I were to move into one of those old homes, the ghost would inhabit my body to search for their lost love in the Louisiana swamps and invariably throw herself to the alligators, with my body, in despair.

I'm also not sure why my lifelong fantasies and dreams seem to have been devoid of the very people who lovingly raised me, but mine were. That probably makes me sound like a horrible human right now. But the truth is I just assumed all would be well and they would forever be that vague "older-than-me" age and living their best lives—in their own antebellum house.

But that's not quite how it turned out. I do not live in an antebellum house and my parents did age into actual old age. I live on a twenty-three-acre property where I reside with my husband, daughter, and mother-in-law in a mountainside-lodge-style house (not on a mountainside); when I stand out front on my non-wraparound porch, I can see where my parents live—a guest house that is exactly sixty-six steps away. (I can also see a barn, three horses, a tractor in the middle of the yard that didn't get put away, and a massive pile of wood and sticks—but that's a story for another time.)

This is what fancy folks call "multigenerational living," and while living all together like this is not as familiar in the United States, it's very common in Latin American and Asian cultures. Can I tell you something? It's wonderful. And apparently, I'm not the only one who thinks so. The number of multigenerational households in the US has increased dramatically in recent years.[9] It's a thing, and it's bound to become a bigger thing. We LOVE it. I never dreamed my life would be this sweet (mostly because, as you know, in my previous dreams my parents didn't quite make the cut).

Living together was my solution to the challenges posed by being a member of the "Sandwich Generation." If you don't already know, this is the group of middle-aged adults who care for both their aging parents and their own children at the same time. Back when everyone was having babies in their early twenties, grandparents were more likely to be in their forties or fifties; this meant that by the time the grandparents needed their grown children to step up and help, those babies had gone off to college or were starting to have their own babies. But we women started increasingly having babies later, our parents became grandparents at an older age, and now many of us find ourselves with children at home and parents in their late seventies and eighties.

Some say we started having babies later because of careers and medicine. I like to think we're the Sandwich Generation women who were really hot for a long time, so we got to have babies later in life. My explanation sounds much better than Wikipedia's.

My sandwich wasn't always served on this twenty-three-acre platter. Before we made this move, Craig and I were both attempting the balance between the daughter in our kitchen and the moms scattered across the country.

In October of 2015, my mother had a brain aneurysm that burst, and by the grace of God, she survived. At the time, my parents lived in Tulsa, Oklahoma—about eight hundred miles from Gulf Breeze, Florida. My mom was in the ICU for a month and then a skilled nursing facility for another three months. I was flying back and forth to Oklahoma, but I still had an eight-year-old at home, and as much as I needed to be there to be an advocate for my mother, I also needed to be a mom to my daughter.

And you know what's even farther than Tulsa? Lancaster, California. That's where Craig's mother, Rosalie, was living. Truthfully, I barely knew my mother-in-law for the first fifteen years of my marriage with Craig. Rosalie suffered from bipolar disorder and it manifested itself in hoarding issues and fears about leaving the house. She also has obsessive-compulsive disorder issues and hated to fly. Because of these issues, she preferred for us not to visit her, and coming to see us meant a very long flight—so she only visited us a handful of times.

It was becoming increasingly clear that for us to be able to give our parents the support we wanted to give, we needed to live closer to them, and with Ella thriving in a small school we adored, that meant the older folks coming to us. First we tried moving Craig's mom to Gulf Breeze, but even when she was just a mile down the road, many of the same challenges remained. We tried getting my parents to move to Gulf Breeze, and although they liked the concept of being closer, the idea of leaving their life of thirty years and finding a new home in Florida felt daunting.

That's when the idea of Trinity was born.

On a fluke one day scrolling on Zillow, I found a stunning twenty-three-acre property about twenty miles north of where we were. It included a main house, a guest house, a horse barn (my daughter rode horses), a large maintenance shed, and even a pond with a water fountain. It was heavenly and just what was needed to push Mom and Dad over the edge to move. We each sold our homes and moved to this glorious property we now call Trinity. I loved the double meaning of the word; we were three entities coming together in our own trinity, and this was a place that honored and cherished the Holy Trinity. It was a perfect name.

Craig and I moved from a 2,200-square-foot home nestled

among a zillion other houses and wonderful neighbors, whose dinnertime conversations I could sometimes hear through their screened windows, to a 4,800-square-foot main house on twenty-three acres (that's about seventeen football fields for any of you who, like pre-2019 me, aren't quite sure what an acre is) in the country—with no neighbors except my own parents in the guest house. (It is not the little hut it might sound like; the guest house is the same size as the neighborhood home Craig and I had just left!)

I'll tell you what's awesome about this in a minute, but first I should clarify: Proximity doesn't mean everything becomes easy—it means the hard stuff becomes easier to get to. We had planned for Craig, Ella, and me to move in first and build an addition for Rosalie once we were settled, because for some reason that huge house had only two bedrooms; the previous owners had grown kids and used the guest house only for guests. But our plans went out the window quickly. Rosalie's health had taken a turn for the worse and we needed to get her in with us right away. Ella got moved to that giant closet.

Everything happened so rapidly with Rosalie. When my mother had her aneurysm, I was at a healthcare facility and surrounded by nurses and experienced therapists and such. But with Rosalie I unexpectedly had to step into the role of caretaker.

With time, we would find the mental space and clarity to acquire long-term support, but as many of you have surely experienced with your own aging parents, sometimes phase one is just about getting through the day. I never had time to mull it over and deeply ponder whether helping Rosalie around the clock was something I was good at or wanted to do; I was thrust into it because it had to be done and there was no time to think. Craig is an only child and is also a pilot who is gone half of every week, so that only left me. I wasn't working outside the home and was in between writing books; all the circumstances stacked up to say, "Hey Dawn, you're it."

I'll admit, caring for your own parents is different from caring for someone you've met only a handful of times in your life. I loved Rosalie because she was the mother of my husband; however, I didn't know her intimately. But let me tell you, we went from zero to "lean that way so I can wipe your bottom" in a very short amount of time.

This wasn't easy for me. Months earlier I'd been a busy entrepreneur darting between large meetings with my team to one-on-one strategy sessions; now I was asking a woman to hold up her breasts so I could clean underneath them. How had I pivoted this hard and fast into something I wasn't even good at? Had God forgotten me or all of the things I was good at? Surely He remembered that I could write and speak and I had a great mind for business. Why wasn't He using me in those ways? Why this, why now?

While it was hard for me to step into this role, it must have been even harder for Rosalie to step into hers. How would it feel to live as a hardworking, proud woman for so long only to have your daughter-in-law, whom you barely know, have to grab you under the arms and pull you up to stand? My heart ached for her.

I want to tell you that it was wonderful to be able to care for Rosalie, and that it was easy, but that'd be a big fat lie. Caring for anyone, no matter how much you love them, is hard. It's physically hard, mentally hard, and, much like parenting, thankless. My mornings would begin with waking her and most of the time changing her clothing and sheets because she had either forgotten to use the restroom or spilled her chocolate Ensure drink all over herself. She was angry when I would wash her, and she hated her showers. No matter how gentle I would be, it would result in Rosalie being angry with me, my clothes soaking wet, and my feeling defeated. All by 11 a.m. Dressing her was difficult because she insisted on wearing only clothing with cats on it or things that were purple. That one always made me laugh a little, because one day when I'm in my eighties, people had better darn well let me dress in cat clothes if I want to. But at the time, getting through those days was hard.

It doesn't mean you don't do it. But it does mean it's hard not to feel resentful and even angry at times. I remember so many times clenching my teeth and saying in my head, *You wrote a chapter in your book called "You Get To"* over and over, trying to convince myself that I GOT to do this. It didn't work. I suspect I was angrier about doing things I thought I was so bad at, like the daily chores of caretaking for another human, than I was about actually taking caring of her. I was angry that the things I perceived as my only gifts in life were not being used; I felt so darn forgotten by the entire world.

I know what you may be thinking: Why didn't we get outside help? Honestly, we were going at warp speed, sort of in this "hang on for dear life" survival mode. I was learning as I went along, trying to figure out how best to care for this fragile eighty-year-old woman, while at the same time both of us were continually stunned by the situation. I couldn't believe this was my life now, and Rosalie couldn't believe she had lost so much of her independence that this woman she barely knew was cleaning her. Craig was managing his full-time job, carrying the emotional load of seeing his mother this way, and trying to handle parenting stuff from an executive lounge in the Houston airport to take the load off me.

Ella was doing her best to make her own lunches and breakfasts, trying to make things easier for me. It was hard for all of us and would have required us coming up for air to rationally think, *Is there a better way to do this?*

After a few months, as Rosalie became stronger and more independent, we did come up for air, and we all agreed that we needed a new solution. I found, through the very scientific way of throwing a pleading post on Facebook about needing help, where I should go. Several friends shared about companies that offered in-home care with nurse's aides. After weeks of searching, we hired a sweet woman named Melodye. She now cares for Rosalie five days a week, six hours a day. She bathes Rosalie, takes walks with her, sits and visits with her, and loves her well. She has been an incredible blessing to our family, and best of all, a sweet new friend to Rosalie.

I want to stop here for a second and fully acknowledge that not everyone has this option. I know that. Rosalie was in a financial position that she could afford to pay for someone to come into our home and help. These things are expensive, and if she hadn't been in a financial position to do it, I would still be caring for her today. But if you do have the option of hiring help, I highly recommend it. It doesn't mean you think you're too important to be your parent's caretaker; it doesn't mean you're outsourcing your love. It means you're sharing the load so that you can use *your* strengths to support your loved ones. It means you have energy left over to just enjoy being together. Later on, my mother suddenly fell ill and was diagnosed with a rare autoimmune disease, Wegener's. Because she and my dad were at Trinity, my dad and I could help each other. I was able to spend four weeks in and out of the hospital being an advocate for my mother, while my dad took Ella to and from school and was around for her in the afternoons when Craig was working. I didn't have to worry that I was neglecting Ella when I just wanted to sit in my mom's hospital room and sing her Michael Bublé songs while I painted her toenails red.

There are blessings and benefits of our close proximity that go infinitely beyond the healthcare realm. Let's take the obvious ones: We never run out of toilet paper. I can always pop next door to Mom and Dad's house and get some. Heck, sometimes I just use their toilet anyway because why dirty up my own if I can borrow theirs, right? There's always someone around to watch and feed the animals, and you never have to worry about waiting around to sign for packages because someone is ALWAYS here. And of course, having five adults pitch in on one mortgage is always nice.

There are some other benefits that go way deeper. Living on a property with my parents and my mother-in-law while we have a young child has been one of the greatest blessings of my life. After years of plane rides, Ella now sees her grandparents every day. She gets to play countless hours of Uno with my mom, laugh with my dad, and room next door to Rosalie, resulting in countless conversations that include "Grandma, can you please turn down the TV?"

Our daughter can sit around a dinner table with her grandparents and her parents and reap the riches of generations. I want her to hear the stories of when they were growing up and the stories of when Craig and I were growing up. I want Ella to understand why we do some of the crazy things we do in our family—like waving like a mad person as our family goes down the driveway and then, right before we lose sight of them, they honk and we all wave really hard one last time. We have done this as long as I can remember. It's so funny and we die laughing every time and . . . okay, maybe you have to be there.

My parents gave me a wild and wonderful and adventurous life growing up. I think Craig would say his mother gave him an equally beautiful childhood, even though she raised him as a single mom from the time he was five years old. We want to be able to give the same back to them at the end of their lives.

I remember about a year ago sitting on my porch in a rocking chair with my parents on the porch swing next to me. Nobody was speaking, they were gently swinging, and Mom was seated closest to me. There wasn't a cloud in the sky, and there was a gentle breeze that made you want to close your eyes and just take in the gloriousness of the outdoors. As I slowly rocked in my chair, I looked over, and I suddenly thought, *One day, they won't be there and this will be a very sad porch.* There will be a day when they all will be gone. I know that this season is sacred, and I want to soak in every part of it.

It wasn't always like this, and it won't always be like this. Any day now, I might find myself back in that round-the-clock caretaking role that I'm so terrible at, and these quiet moments of appreciation might be replaced with my late-night tears of exhaustion and overwhelm.

That's what comes with being part of the Sandwich Generation. I know from speaking with so many of you that my experiences of being unexpectedly thrust into a caretaking role are familiar. But I also know that, despite how common this is, we're not talking about it nearly enough. Some of that is because to talk about it, you have to have the time to have a conversation. But some of it, I think, is because of all the guilt and sadness that comes with this topic.

Some of you reading might feel guilt or sadness because you don't have the capacity to support your aging parents. You can't even make it to their house once a month, let alone buy a weird commune together out in the sticks. Or the demands of your own life are too overwhelming, or you live in a different state, or your relationship with your parents is too strained. Maybe the bottom slice of your sandwich is struggling in school and you just can't give the top slice the attention it needs. (Am I taking the sandwich metaphor too far?)

And there are many of you, I am sure, who are at the other end of the spectrum. You're feeling guilty and sad because you're putting your own family's lives and needs on hold to help an aging parent get through just one more day. You probably also feel utterly exhausted and somewhat resentful—which makes you feel guilty too!

Whether helping your aging parents is working out wonderfully or is a constant source of tears, it's important we talk about it. It's hard. But talking can also be a path to gaining ridiculously simple ideas we are too worn out to think of on our own. Your talking might look like mine and come in the form of a desperate plea on social media, or it might mean raising the topic among your close friends. Either way, you'll quickly discover the Sandwich Generation got its own cute name because there are so many of us, and you'll be shocked at how many have been where you are and want to help guide you. Ask for help. The world is your deli.

Fifteen

All About the Benjamins

Never Give Up Your Financial Power

*I*n a future book, I'd like to write a chapter on finances that focuses on how to deplete them rapidly because (*she says humbly*) I am very good at this. I can take your $1,000,000 investment to $500,000 in no time. And I'm not talking about splurging on diamond-encrusted flip-flops and caviar tacos. Just set me loose in a Target soft furnishings department and I can get through a whole paycheck in minutes. If it were up to me, I'd have everyone buying throw pillows for every season and holiday, no matter how much money was in the bank account. Throw pillows are ALWAYS a good decision in my mind.

But this is a chapter about financial empowerment. It's less about asking where your money *goes* and more about asking, *Do you know where your money is?*

You'll notice a lot of this chapter is aimed at those of you who are married—or anyone whose finances are intertwined with those of another person. Single women already know much of what I'm going to say because they've always managed their own finances. (In fact, y'all could probably write this chapter better than I can, but I believe there will be a few nuggets in here you'll find useful anyway.)

Let me tell you why I ask if you know where your money is. About five years ago I was sitting at a charming little Mexican restaurant, devouring the free chips and queso. Wait, correction, I had to *buy* the queso, it wasn't free—see, I know where my money goes—because God made me in such a way that I cannot eat a tortilla chip without it being smothered in queso. (I consider queso to be one of God's great blessings on my life.) I was with my dear friend, whom I'll call Sally. (Her name has been changed to protect me, the innocent, from her kicking my heinie for sharing this.) Between the queso-dripped chips and mango margaritas, Sally and I began talking about our finances, a topic we've always openly discussed because our husbands are in the same industry with similar earnings, so we both feel there's nothing to hide.

On that particular day, we talked about the things we spent too much money on, like outdoor furniture and, of course, outdoor pillows. Yes, both are stupidly expensive but you *have* to get the expensive stuff so it lasts; otherwise, you're buying new stuff every year. Somehow our deep conversation about outdoor furniture moved into a deeper conversation about retirement and how much we thought it would take to live on once our husbands were forced to retire at sixty-five.

We were on the same page at that point, brainstorming our needs and wants (and debating which category queso fits into), but then I started moving us away from how much money we should have toward how much money we *actually* have, and suddenly it wasn't such a two-way conversation.

I could see Sally's expression shift uncomfortably and I wasn't sure why. Had I said too much? Was she scared to tell me that Craig and I needed ten times what I thought we did? I decided to stop talking and dig back into the queso. The next words that came out of Sally's mouth made my jaw drop so far that little birds could have come and made little cheese nests in my mouth.

"I actually have no idea how much we have in retirement," Sally said. "Jim is the only one with access to it."

I was flabbergasted. How could she not know this about her life? Did she really not know if they had $80 million or $80?

I know what you're thinking: Sally is one of those meek, submissive, wallflower types that say things like "Well gosh, I really have no idea about such things, it's just so confusing for little ol' me." Trust me, she's not at all. She's a strong, vibrant, smart woman and has been married for over thirty years to a wonderful man who respects her and seems to treat her as his equal in all ways. All of this added to my complete state of shock.

I pushed a little more, wanting to understand how this could possibly be, how it was that she didn't know any information about her financial situation for the future. She looked confused at first, as if my questions were a bit dramatic and I was overreacting. But then, in about the amount of time it took for me to order another round of mangoritas, her furrowed brow (yes, Botox is on the future "needs" list) started to relax and she leaned back in her seat, nodding with new understanding. It *was* strange, she admitted to me, that she knew so little about their financial situation. Then, sitting at this little Mexican restaurant with a fresh yellow-orange drink in her perfectly manicured fifty-five-year-old hand, Sally said, "I'm going to fix this."

She later told me how she called her husband on the way home from the restaurant and asked why she didn't have access to anything, and why she hadn't seen statements or accounts. According to Sally, she was ready to launch into a long explanation of why she needed to be involved and why he needed to stop keeping her in the dark, but it turns out that wasn't necessary. He jumped at the chance to share everything with her; he wanted her to be part of the decision-making. It wasn't that he had been hiding something or thought her incapable of handling this knowledge; it was just that she had never asked.

Comfortable or not, we must be an active participant in our own financial future.

Now, don't get all your feathers in a ruffle; I am not saying you have to manage it all. If you are not knowledgeable about your family's finances, my guess is it's simply because you and your partner long ago divided up the physical and cognitive loads of your life together and the money stuff landed on his to-handle list. The last thing you want is to take on one. more. thing. But I AM saying you should know what is going on. You should have access to it, understand it, know where all the money is, and how to get to it should anything happen.

And don't you dare let yourself think thoughts like *I'm not smart enough to do this.* You ARE smart enough. I mean, you're reading this book, right? This is a huge indicator of your brilliance. But you are not (brace yourself) allowed to bury your head in the sand because it's easier to let someone do it than it is to face up to the reality of a few spreadsheets and financial statements. No ma'am.

Okay, you have my full permission to throw the book now, but pick it back up in the next five minutes because I've got some good stuff up next.

Oh hey, welcome back. Let's get started.

Now listen, I'm not an expert on money matters, and you weren't looking for a financial adviser when you bought this book. So, I'm going to keep my tips nice and simple, and then I'm going to go back to what I do best: telling tenuously related stories about other women in my life. With that said, here is a little checklist of simple, essential first steps you can take toward financial empowerment:

- Make a list of all your bank accounts and their logins. There are great apps out there today that will save all your passwords in one place. You can add people in the program to share all the information should anything happen to you. I personally use LastPass.

- After knowing and documenting all your accounts, do the same for investment accounts and retirement accounts. Make note of what is in these accounts and take steps to understand whether you are on track to be where you want to be for retirement. Don't hesitate to schedule a session with a financial consultant, especially one who comes personally recommended by friends or family.

- Make a list of all insurance policies—home, life, auto, health, pet, all of them. Know the companies, your representatives, and how to log in to your accounts. You want to make sure that everything is up-to-date. Review your coverage, payouts, and beneficiaries. Understand how to access the money you need if anything should happen to you or your spouse.

- Have your name on the utility bill and at least one other bill. If you're married or have long lived with friends or family, there's a chance your name isn't on anything. If the unexpected happens and you find yourself on your own trying to start anew, it can be shockingly difficult to prove your identity or credit without bills in your name.
- Make sure you are on the title to your home. You do not need to be on the mortgage but you certainly want to make sure you're on the title. This is the same for your car; make sure your name is on the title.
- Pull your credit report. It is good to know what is on it, if there are any hits against you, and where you stand. Remember, knowledge is power.

How do you feel when you see that list?

Some of you are probably like "Duh, thanks for wasting my time, Dawn. I know all this." To you, I say, rock on, sister.

Some of you are probably like Sally. All it takes is somebody posing the question over some queso to make you pause and think, *Yeah, I need to fix that.*

For others, though, you're still thinking money stuff just isn't in your wheelhouse and you're fine with that. But nope. That's not fine. We're not talking about dirty laundry and getting boxes out of the attic. Maybe your partner doesn't know which little slot holds the liquid Tide, and maybe you've been feigning a back injury for twenty-five years to avoid being the one who gets out the Christmas decorations, and *that* is fine. If one of you is suddenly out of the picture, everybody can still get through the day. He'll google the make and model of the washing machine, or you'll sigh heavily and get yourself up into the darn attic. (And yes, those examples are pretty sexist, and to be honest, I don't even do the laundry and I love going into the attic. But you get my point.)

That's not the case with financial information. Your financial situation can't be something only one of you knows about. You could suddenly lose your partner—whether through divorce, death, dingoes, infidelity, or an incapacitating illness—and if you don't have access to anything but a credit card and a few twenties in your purse, you're in trouble. You can't google your way into your partner's life insurance policy. You can't move yourself into a single lady's condo and just hope someone's going to pay for it. You can't sell your car if you don't know where the title is.

The same holds true if you're single or divorced. You can't be the only person who knows all of this key information. If a house fire takes all the printed versions of your key documents, or you're the one who becomes incapacitated, it's essential that somebody else knows where to look and how to access information about your insurances and finances. This could be a trusted loved one or a professional; just make sure you've made clear instructions available in anticipation of the unanticipated happening.

Let me tell you another little story that might help me explain myself and my seemingly harsh words a little more. I have an amazing friend named Candie (not her real name). When she was thirty-five, she was divorced and had two daughters. Financially she was fine—not loaded, but she had her ducks in a row. Then she fell in love and remarried. This man was very wealthy, and because he'd had lots of money before she came along, Candie didn't feel she had the right to ask about finances or even see any of their information.

During the handful of times she did ask, he dismissed her. Almost like a pat on the head, telling her to go back in her room and play. Now, we come from a long line of women who don't handle being dismissed particularly well, so she pushed more. She wanted to understand what to do if anything were to happen to him—what were the accounts, the passwords, or even the names of the companies with which they had accounts. She had absolutely no idea. But he always pushed back, told her not to worry and to just "call our accountant" if anything happened. So she quit pushing. She was busy mothering five kids—her own two plus his three—through middle and high school, for goodness' sake, plus she felt safe and believed she would always be taken care of.

You can probably guess where this is going. After fifteen years of marriage, they divorced. It was a very not-amicable divorce, and for reasons that surpass anything I can attempt to explain, Candie suddenly found herself fifty years old and practically broke. It was only then that she realized how little she was entitled to, and since she had spent their marriage doing the unending but unpaid work of keeping their huge household functioning, she had no savings that were "hers." Worse, due partly to being kept in the dark about family finances over the preceding years, she had no strategy for ensuring future stability for her and her daughters.

I share this because I want you to know how quickly things can change and how burying our heads in the sand can devastate us financially. Candie was blindsided by it all.

Now, the good part of this story is that Candie did go on to be a ridiculously successful artist and teacher and now makes beaucoup money. But it was a distressing position to be in, to say the least. Today, I promise she knows where every single penny of her money is and her name is on EVERYTHING.

Women find themselves locked outside of their own financial worlds for any number of reasons. Sometimes it's easier to feel safe and not ask questions than it is to take off the rose-colored glasses. Honestly, I think this is the case with many of us. Some of us are just math-avoidant. Single, divorced, married, widowed—whatever our circumstances, we just don't want to dive into the numbers. It can be intimidating and it's not exactly fun. (I mean, unless you're one of those spreadsheet aficionados. I know you're out there.) Plus, we're busy enough just keeping an eye on what comes in and what goes out each month. And I know that for some married women, it's easy to assume if their husband is the main breadwinner in the family, then he gets to dictate what happens with the family's financial future. (My friend, if you need my speech on why non-monetary contributions to a relationship are just as valuable—if not more valuable—than the dollars coming in, call me.)

I'll admit it. I've worn the cute rose-colored glasses. For many years, every time Craig and I did anything involving mortgages, like buying or selling a property, I'd completely shut down and say things like "Oh, that's Craig's area." Why was it his area? I was just as capable of picking up a phone and talking to our mortgage broker and asking her to explain it all to me. But I literally played dumb and acted like a child. I'm embarrassed to say that I didn't even try to understand; instead I just trusted that Craig had the whole thing under control.

And I'll admit that I'm not exactly diving into the middle of it now either. Of course, each of us has different strengths that we bring to a relationship, and if Craig takes joy in comparing APRs, who am I to stand in his way? But I peek over his shoulder now. I ask questions and make it clear I'd like to hear his thought process and to be involved in making the final decisions. And, most importantly, I make sure that (a) I'm involved in signing all the paperwork and (b) I know exactly how to access said paperwork.

This is about making sure YOU know where YOU are. This is not about you taking classes in finances and getting your investor's certificate (that's what it's called, right?). I just want you to understand where you are.

And PLEASE hear me: For those of you sharing your finances with a partner, I am not saying all men are deceitful or are trying to hide something. Not at all. In fact, I suspect that most men are trying to be good and caring husbands and take care of their family in the ways that were modeled to them by their fathers and grandfathers. If you think about it, we are only one generation away from a time when men handled all the financials because women weren't allowed to have bank accounts without a man's signature. We could not get a loan, a credit card, or a car without a man's signature. No really, it's true. That still blows my mind a little.

We fought for these rights and this independence, so why aren't we participating more in our own financial freedoms? Why aren't we making sure our name is on the title of the car or the house? Why don't we have logins to all the accounts and know where the money is?

We have raised a generation of strong, faith-filled, fierce women, and yet our actions are not matching our words. We tell them to be independent and to chase their dreams, but we model that someone else will handle all the money—as if to say, don't worry your pretty little head about it, someone else will handle that.

I am making a big generalization here, and not every woman does this. Many of us do participate actively in our financial futures. I'm the person who handles the day-to-day finances in my own home (probably not a super smart call on Craig's part, but at least we have throw pillows). But I feel compelled to talk about this because too many times I've heard what almost sounds like pride from women saying things like "Oh you know, Mike handles all that stuff. I have no idea."

HAVE AN IDEA. Having no idea is not okay.

Let me give you one last way to look at this. I once learned a goal-setting exercise when I was in my twenties and working in sales for a radio station. Obviously it didn't mean much to me because I was in my twenties and I knew everything. But luckily I experienced it again in my forties. This time, the exercise was guided by a woman speaking at an event, and she shared it in a beautiful way that really stuck with me.

This is what she told us:

Imagine you're eighty years old and you are happy.

Where are you sitting?

Who is sitting next to you?

Are you in a house, a condo, or maybe a retirement community?

What is your view?

Who is there with you? Is it your children, your grandchildren, your friends?

Now reflect on what you just imagined. In order to be where you visualized your eighty-year-old self, what do you need to be doing now?

Start with your body. What do you need to do for your health to ensure that you make it to that age?

Now let's move to who you are with. Who's sitting next to you? Who's coming by to visit later? How can you foster those relationships now to ensure in the future you'll be surrounded by those you love? For me, I want to be surrounded by my family. My children and their children. My friends and their children whom I love like my own. Your dream might involve clinking champagne glasses with your besties, or having nothing but a book and a coffee at your side.

Now focus on where you are. My imagined picture always involves the back porch of a small house on a lake with Craig by my side. You might go with somewhere a little more glamorous, like a luxury penthouse in Paris, or more serene, like one of those idyllic huts in the Maldives. So what do our finances need to look like today to ensure that we can live in that picture when we retire?

Sometimes it is easier to assess our lives backward rather than writing down our next five-year plan. Both are important, but capturing a visual of what you want near the end of your life and working backward from that can be beautifully motivating.

If you have a partner, now you have to run through this same exercise together. Where do your pictures overlap? Where do they differ? Talk about this together.

Either way, the next step is to put on a pot of coffee, find your favorite notepad, and settle down in front of the computer. It's time to look at the finances.

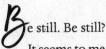

Sixteen

Hello, God, Remember Me?

The Quiet Seasons of Change Are Seasons of the Most Significant Growth

> *Be still, and know that I am God!*
> (Psalm 46:10)

Be still. Be still?

It seems to me that if God knew He would be calling me to the occasional seasons of "being still" throughout my life, He would have thrown in a dash or two of meditating monk vibes when creating my inner spirit. Instead, I have the inner workings of an unfocused hyperactive squirrel bouncing from tree to tree, trying to rally my fellow tree-hopping rodent friends for the next great adventure.

If God KNEW what my life would hold—and He does—then why create me in such a way that is the polar opposite of what He calls me to do? Why call me to write books when it is so hard for me? Why not give that calling to the girl down the street who has journaled every day of her life, makes long, detailed lists for what she will do that day, and takes meticulous notes at church and parent-teacher meetings? That girl loves and thrives on the written word.

God has a thing for choosing those who feel, and even are, unqualified. When God calls us to things we don't understand or to things that feel foreign and difficult to us, it's no mistake. There is always a lesson and blessin' in it. (Okay, too much?) What I mean to say is that when He puts us through particularly challenging things, something good always comes out of it—if we let it.

One of my most difficult callings was simply to "be still" or, as I like to call it, to endure a season of agonizing-directionless-hushed-stillness.

Awhile back, God called me—or shall I say dragged me—into a period of agony that lasted for what I thought was about eighty-seven years, though when I consulted the calendar I could see it was more like a year and a half. I know I keep saying "called me," so let me explain that a little.

We all "hear" God in different ways, but for me, I mostly hear Him in the voice of my mind, in a gut feeling, or in the occasional dream. Trying to articulate to others why you *know* something is from God is downright hard. I *know* when God is calling me into something and when He isn't. But telling others how we know it's Him is challenging, especially when we doubt ourselves at every turn.

But in this case, for this season, it was the opposite of hearing a "calling." My mind, my gut, and my dreams were completely devoid of a call to action or a nudge to move. In fact it was devoid of anything at all, and the only thing I felt from God over and over and over was Him saying, "Be still." Which was ridiculous. He couldn't make me the way He did and then ask me to be still; it was a contradiction, a conflict of interest. Surely He meant this message for anyone else but me.

But no matter how hard I prayed and how much I fought it, I heard nothing but the utterly absurd "be still" with the occasional "and know that I am God."

There are times when God feels so relatable and responsive that I can pull up a chair and have coffee with Him and have a deep, detailed discussion about why He made peonies (my favorite flower next to hydrangeas) so beautiful but does not let them grow or bloom in the panhandle of Florida. Or why He made sugar so sweet and delicious, but it's bad for the very bodies He created. Other days I feel closer on a more visceral level, like I can just place my head on His lap, close my eyes, and let His gentle hand glide over my hair—and with each stroke comes a promise that everything is perfect. I hear Him again and again, day after day, and experiencing that closeness makes just about anything possible because, after all, God is with me. It wouldn't matter if I were changing a tire on a car (well, making the phone call and then standing nearby offering helpful suggestions to whoever showed up to help me) or writing a book—He is there and all things are possible.

But what happens when we don't feel the closeness of God? What happens when the only thing we feel Him saying to us is "be still," or worse, when we don't hear Him at all? If you're me, you cry. A lot. And you get depressed, change into your 1998 gray-striped Walmart nightgown accented with numerous holes of varying sizes created from 789 washings, crawl into bed, and watch countless hours of ridiculous TV and pout.

However, even I can only pout for so long. When I found myself several months into the season of agonizing-directionless-hushed-stillness, I knew I needed to dig a little deeper into what *being still* actually meant.

But first, let me set the stage for what was happening at that time. I was one year out from my big million-dollar year with Mary Kay, which meant I was six months out from my resignation from that company. I had gone from chasing big monthly goals and working with a large team of women to working with, and for, a party of one: me. And just between us, she was incredibly difficult.

My first book was completed and in the hands of the publisher for final touches on design before getting sent off to be printed overseas; the next stage was for me to wait almost a year before its release date. Craig and I had just moved with our parents out to the country, which was thirty minutes from all our friends, stores, and favorite restaurants. To top it all off, I had stepped into the unexpected role of caretaker to my mother-in-law.

Life was completely different than it had been six months earlier. For the first time in many, many years, I wasn't working. I was managing things at Trinity and caring for parents but felt as if none of my giftings were being used. I was desperate to hear from God, desperate for guidance on the next big calling. *How about another book, or a business, or great idea to run with? Give me anything, God, just anything.* Months earlier God had been so clear in my life and guided me all the way through from the idea of the book to finding an agent, a publisher, a new dream home, and so many other things. I had not only felt Him walk beside me in that season, but it was almost as if He was holding my hand tightly as we went through those days together. And now, I felt as if His fingers had unraveled from mine, and I was alone.

Despite all that God had done for me, not just with the book but with my whole life—His love for me during the loss of my child, my rape, the cancer, and so much more—I was so quick to wonder if He had suddenly forgotten me. I was a little like the Israelites coming out of Egypt. They had just witnessed *insanely* awesome miracles from God, camping at the base of a mountain where God was at the top, and yet they decided to make a golden cow to worship. Okay, maybe I wasn't that bad, but I was close.

But God hadn't forgotten me. In fact, looking back, now I can tell you that it was one of the most precious times of my life, and God showed His love for me in such a deep and profound way that it set my life on course for something beautiful.

Let me explain. Have you ever been around a child, a teen, or even an adult who is really tired and refuses to admit it? They see things negatively, they don't reason well, and everything seems so much worse and heavier than it really is? But you know, as you're watching this tired child/adult, that if they would just go to bed and rest for a little while, the entire world would be different to them when they wake up.

That's us. Sometimes what we need more than anything is rest. When we have these seasons when God calls us to be still, it is because He knows us even better than we know ourselves. He loves us so much that He wants us to stop and to rest. And not just rest, but to rest IN HIM.

Did you know that God loves us so much that He literally commands us to rest? He created the Sabbath, an actual day of rest in the commandments, which most Christians today acknowledge as Sunday. The Bible says He "blessed the Sabbath day and set it apart as holy" (Exodus 20:11). He commands you to rest and He knows exactly how much time you need; He knows how many days you need to be still and rest in Him to replenish your worn-out, broken, and tired body and mind.

Now, admittedly it took me a while to figure this out. But after many months of agonizing-directionless-hushed-stillness, I began to grow weary from resisting the silence and instead began stepping into it. I learned that I needed to begin every single morning by verbally surrendering my day to God. I'm sure you have a vision of some angelic being in flowing white robes falling elegantly to her knees and crying out, "I surrender it all to You, God!" as tears glisten on her long, naturally thick eyelashes. Close. Or not close at all. It was more like me and that Walmart gown waking up, yawning, rolling to my back, and croaking through my morning breath, "Good morning, God. I love You, and I surrender every part of this day to You." It's a small thing, but it's significant and symbolic that the first of my day goes to Him.

Admittedly, quickly thereafter I'm off to the bathroom, and I then settle into my favorite chair for some coffee and a good social media scroll. But those first moments, before my feet even hit the floor, are His.

I'm not one of those people who always does things the way we think the perfect Christian Bible-studying girl does. I don't wake up before everyone, study His Word, and pray for an hour before beginning my day. I wish it looked like that, but it doesn't always work for me. Often it's not till later in my day that I find the quiet space to fully give Him my attention. But I do want to learn, and I want to understand more about His Word, always. I try to find the studies that work well for me and the wild way I tend to do life. Flexible studies that give me a little grace, if you will. I used to think if I didn't care for a particular study, there was something wrong with me, that I was not "Christian" enough, but I learned over the years to just seek out the ones that resonate with me. If it doesn't speak to me, I keep looking.

There is a wonderful program called Bible Study Fellowship that's been around for a gazillion years, and it's an amazing program done all over the world. One book of the Bible is taught per year, and you and a group study that book together for the whole twelve months. You do daily readings and studies on your own and then connect with your group weekly to go over it. It's an intense Bible study, and a beautiful one. But I first signed up to do one of those in a season of my life that was wild and crazy, and I repeatedly missed our Thursday groups. The more I missed, the more I felt like a failure as I fell increasingly behind. Please know that feeling of failing is NOT of God. God loves you whether you do it no minutes a day or hours a day. God wants you to seek Him always, but God totally, utterly, and ridiculously loves you. Always, no matter what. With all your flaws, faults, and bad scheduling, He loves you.

I'm saying this to you because I believe that in our seasons of rest, He isn't just calling us to rest but to rest in Him. That means actively pursuing Him more than ever. That's a hard thing to do when you're a mere mortal with Instagram.

In addition to starting my day surrendered to Him and finding a flexible way to be in His Word, I realized I felt a little closer to God when I was in nature. I love to be in nature—not hiking or anything crazy, but when I walk around outside, I see God so vividly in the colorful birds flying from tree to tree or in the vibrance of blooming shades of yellows and pinks. I feel Him in the wind that brushes over my face and in the sun when it kisses my cheeks. I see God in such an abundant way in nature, and because of this I try to get outside—a lot.

In that season I also learned to create a playlist of worship music I can listen to when I walk in nature. I learned to schedule time to be with God, the way I would with a good friend for a walk or a visit on the porch. (Only, His schedule is always clear for me, which makes it a lot easier to coordinate.) Not only is God worth it, but I am also worth it. I am worth being still for, and taking a walk with. I am worth sitting on a swing and quietly taking it all in.

One of my most important lessons learned during this season of stillness was that my self-worth was not tied to an accolade or a paycheck. It didn't matter if I spoke on stages or wrote bestselling books or devoted half my day to my mother-in-law's ablutions. I was fully whole, simply because I was His. He taught me that all my most precious gifts were right in front of me, and honestly, that nothing else mattered. In this season of frustration with God for not giving me the next wild and wonderful dream to chase or the next big thing to focus on, I did find something. I found myself.

I know what some of you are thinking. You wish you had time, just five minutes, to sit and crash on your sofa because your schedule may be so full. And perhaps this is not a season in which He is calling you to rest in Him; perhaps this is the season that your blessings are flowing. Or perhaps you're coming to an end of this season and your time of rest is nearly upon you. My time of rest didn't come at some self-perceived ideal time. I didn't look at my life calendar and think, *Okay, and then we're going to take about two years off right here.* In fact, it was quite the opposite. I was told I was going to rest *now*—not in a couple of months, not in a couple of years, but right now. Everything would stop and all that I would hear from Him would be to "be still and rest in me." *Be still.*

One day, after learning to cherish the season I was in, after learning to love the woman He made me to be, with or without achievement, His next callings on my life began flooding through my mind. A clear outline and idea for the next book, retreats for women, and working with Melissa. I would not have been ready for any of them had I not taken the time to stop and replenish a dry and weary woman.

God has miracles in store for you. He has blessings coming for you that you can't possibly imagine or fathom. But He needs you ready for those blessings. He needs you ready for the next thing, and in order for that to happen, you need rest. You need to recharge, and you need to pour into your soul, your mind, and your body. Remember, a season of rest is not because you are forgotten or He doesn't love you; it's because He does love you.

"He cuts off every branch of mine that doesn't produce fruit, and he prunes the branches that do bear fruit so they will produce even more" (John 15:2).

There are times in our lives that almost feel as if we are in our own little winter. A cold, hard season of feeling bare. As if everything about you is hard and frozen and there is no way you can grow anything, let alone bloom or shine again. You feel dry and weary like a brittle branch. Sometimes we become so familiar with these feelings that we believe this is normal; this is life. But God knows better and knows what we need, even when we don't. He knows that seasons of rest and being still are like water to the dry places of our souls. He will water your dry bones so you may come alive again, I promise you.

Seventeen

Drop the Box

Forgiveness and Releasing Bitterness

From the age of nine, my husband, Craig, knew that he wanted to be a pilot when he grew up. He set the course and he stuck to it—excellent grades, ROTC, then Marines, then Cobra pilot, then airline pilot for the big boys. He never once wavered on that path.

I, on the other hand, wavered like a drunk trying to walk a straight line down Bourbon Street at Mardi Gras. And my vision of my future was as clear as the murky bayou waters surrounding that fine city of New Orleans. I had a lot of jobs and hobbies and interests (heck, I still do). I felt like God kept giving me new gifts to unravel and step into every few years, and it took me years to recognize what I was good at and what I wasn't. But finally, at fifty-two years old, I found the job of my dreams.

I know what you're thinking: It's this "authory" thing.

Actually, that's not it. Writing is not particularly easy for me, and while I love the finished product, I definitely struggle through the process. Yes, I'm also a speaker, and while I have a ball doing it and acknowledge that I am gifted in this area (can I say that without sounding full of myself?), it still pales in comparison to what I love the most.

What I love most is working toe-to-toe, face-to-face, with women. I love being a small part of a journey of reminding them how magnificent they are. These days that is accomplished through the Retreat at Trinity, an intimate gathering of women five times a year. I have the privilege of bringing women into my home for three days at a time and watching them go through a life-changing transformation.

It is humbling to witness such dramatic life change in a woman during such a short amount of time. But their change is so big that it is physically obvious. We take photos of each participant shortly after their arrival and then again two days later. Their beautiful transformation is evident in every photo.

So what can happen over three days to have an impact so strong that it's visible? We're not juicing or doing face-lifts or dermabrasion over here. I haven't pulled an Oprah and hidden the keys to a new car under each person's resin wicker rocking chair. Yes, everyone sleeps well and eats *really* well, and for some women, spending three days among fellow amazing women laughing and crying and discussing deep, meaningful ideas is enough to elicit the lightness that appears by Sunday afternoon.

But for many, what you're seeing in those "after" photos is forgiveness—including forgiveness of oneself.

Working so closely with women for so many years, first in direct sales and now in this far more intimate way, I have seen certain patterns and circumstances repeated with women from all walks of life. When women are feeling deeply stuck and having a hard time moving forward in their lives, there are countless reasons, but there is often one common denominator: They are battling with Unforgiveness. And Unforgiveness often brings his little friend Bitterness. The deep heaviness of these two burdens, bitterness and unforgiveness, will prevent any person from fully flourishing in their life.

Holding on to bitterness and unforgiveness is a little like carrying a large box in your arms—at least it was that way for me after a year of unfathomable pain and trauma. I've shared that I lost my daughter Madison unexpectedly to a rare bacterial pneumonia when she was nine months old. Three months later my first husband, Allan, and I separated, and three months after that separation, a man broke into my home and raped me. My box was filled with so much rage at God, my rapist, and my soon-to-be ex-husband. At first I barely noticed the box; I was an angry, bitter disaster of a human, so the box felt just right, and my raging adrenaline made it easy for me to carry it.

I carried that box of unforgiveness wrapped with tissue papers of bitterness day after day. But as the days and years went by and I started going through the motions of a normal, functioning human, its heaviness increased. That box was coming between me and a healthy life, but I was so used to carrying it that it didn't even occur to me to put it down. I let it stop me from having flourishing dating relationships after my divorce, and my friendships and relationships with my family were also strained. Worst of all, it simply stopped me from moving forward. I was stuck with that stupid box.

It took me a long while, but I eventually started to realize that

I could put the box down. So I did. I laid that box down at the feet of God Himself. But for some dumb reason, I picked it up again. And then the same thing happened over the next few years; I'd put it down and pick it up again and again and again. Apparently I'm not the only person in history to do this. In fact, there's a verse in the Bible showing Peter asking Jesus about this very thing:

"Lord, how often should I forgive someone who sins against me? Seven times?"

"No, not seven times," Jesus replied, "but seventy times seven!" (Matthew 18:21–22)

Jesus says seventy times seven—not meaning that we need to walk up to a person and say "I forgive you" that many times; that doesn't really change our hearts too much, does it? He knows we are human and how we are wired. He knows that we will pick up that box over and over and over, and He's telling us to hand it over to Him as many times as it takes to finally leave it at His feet. He's telling YOU to let it go over and over and over.

I had to make a conscious and continual decision to stop carrying that box. I had not forgotten what had happened, or what had been done to me that night when a stranger broke into my home, but I was tired, and I finally understood that I could give all of that—every single bit of it—to God.

We might think forgiveness is about the other person, and our getting to a point where we can say, "Dude, it's all good. We're cool." Well, that feels utterly undoable. We've endured great wrongs against us by another person and the world says we should just shake it off? We should just move on? That is NOT what I am saying.

What I am saying is that we are only making ourselves suffer when we decide to stay locked into a place of anger, carrying our heavy box of unforgiveness rather than setting it down and moving forward.

Let me lay it out real clearly for you now: Forgiving is what allows us to move forward. Read that line again. *Forgiving is what allows us to move forward.*

This is a powerful insight, but it typically doesn't sink in quickly or easily. That's why I'm going to keep talking about it for another two thousand words or so. Hang with me—it's worth it.

Our shoulders are not wide enough, our backs strong enough, or our hearts big enough to carry boxes filled with heaviness. We are not meant to lug around the pains and anger over the loss of a child or years of abuse or the wrongs of a spouse or a family member or friend. And we are not meant to carry so much shame and unforgiveness toward ourselves. The truth is, more often than you might ever expect, the anger inside the box isn't due to the actions of others. Sometimes the box is filled with unforgiveness for the person in the mirror.

I'm going to tell you a story, and it's probably going to freak you out a little. Melissa—you know, the biblically brilliant, physically stunning thing who works with me—has told this story around me several times, and each time I get chills. It's such an extraordinary reminder that we need to . . . well, I won't spoil it for you—just keep reading.

Many years ago, when Melissa was in her midtwenties, she joined a group from her school to go on a revival mission trip to a church in Mexico. The purpose of their trip was simply to bring joy and excitement to these churches again, a revival of sorts. On their second night, the group joined the locals for a church service. It was a little white church with old wooden pews, a simple cross at the front of the sanctuary, and just a basic stand for the pastor to speak from. Nothing fancy, just beautiful simplicity.

That night the church service was led by Melissa's pastor, Ben, and all the members of Melissa's group were sprinkled around the locals in attendance. Ben delivered a powerful and exciting sermon in Spanish (Melissa also speaks Spanish), and at the end he asked for anyone in the audience who would like prayer to stand up so others could pray over them. Directly in front of Melissa, a woman stood up. It was clear by the way the woman was crying and shaking that something was deeply hurting her.

Melissa stood and placed her hands on the woman and asked gently how she could pray for her. The woman turned around with tears flowing down her face and said, "I hear voices." Melissa placed her hands on the woman and said, "We ask that these voices leave in Jesus' name." But as soon as she prayed these words aloud, the woman began to shake all over. Seriously. (I told you it was going to get a little freaky.) Now this is where I probably would have hightailed it out of that church, but Melissa is . . . well, Melissa. Instead, she turned to Ben and asked for help. Ben calmly came over and saw what was happening, then he looked at Melissa and said, "She's possessed by a demon and it comes through as sin. She needs to walk through forgiveness."

Melissa asked when she had begun to hear voices, and the woman explained that it was when she began working for a drug dealer in California. She never took the drugs, the woman said, but she did transport them. When that started, so did the voices.

Melissa walked the woman through forgiving the people who got her into the drug business. After listing and actively forgiving the drug dealers by name, the demon was still present. So together they moved to listing members of her family and then others in her life. But even after doing all of this for at least an hour, it was evident there was still a demon.

Finally, when Melissa thought she had gone through everyone, the young woman quietly whispered, "I forgive myself."

There was an immediate and overwhelming peace. The woman began weeping and praising God. Did you catch that? Forgiving *herself* was a critical part of what released that demon.

There may be offenses against you, but sometimes it's the offense against yourself that needs to be released for full freedom. I told y'all it was a crazy story. (And it's even more powerful to hear Melissa tell it.)

I understand that many people will read that story with a skeptical, squinted-eyes head tilt that says, "Ummmm . . . I'm not so sure I buy into that." I get it. I might be skeptical, too, if I hadn't heard it from Melissa herself. But even if you're not comfortable with the idea of demons among us, surely you can believe that a woman would be wrought with pain over unrealized guilt. Many of you reading have probably been that woman.

Let me share another story. A more subtle one, one that doesn't involve Hollywood levels of drama but rather a quiet revelation.

Have you ever met one of those deep, existential-thinking, profound-speaking people who come up with brilliant new thoughts and ideas all on their own? Well, I am NOT one of them. My bestie Kali is, though, and just between us, it's downright annoying. I suspect that 99 percent of the world's content that is put out there is basically the same ol' stuff told again in a slightly different way. But not Kali. She is actually one of seven people left in the world who actually births new ideas and thoughts on a regular basis.

Not long ago, Kali returned from speaking at a large

conference in Nashville, and I asked her what she'd been focusing on. She told me that weeks before the trip, she'd had an epiphany (of course she did) that had completely changed the way she thought about women and confidence. She said, "I think our confidence today comes from three places: our past, our present, and our future."

Okay, I thought. Interesting. But it was when she elaborated on the part about the past that her idea hit me like a ton of bricks. She said, "I realized that instead of letting our past go, we need to simply let it be. Not let it go, but let it be."

I thought about it. In fact, I thought about it deeply. (I guess I have it in me after all.) What would it be like if we just let it be rather than let it go? I don't know how to just "let go" that a strange man broke into my house and raped me while my sleeping toddler was only steps away. But I do know how to let that be and give it to God. One sounds much easier than the other, doesn't it? To me, letting something go seems hard. It seems like clenched hands and whitened knuckles negotiating with my past. *Letting it be* sounds like a release, an acknowledgment of what it is but still choosing to just set it down and walk away. We're still able to see it, we still know it's there, but we're choosing to let it be and put the unforgiveness, bitterness, and anger at the feet of Jesus.

What would it be like if we just set down that box containing all our stories of tragedy and hurt and bitterness? What if we simply put it down and kept walking? We know that they are there, we know that we can go back to them, but for now, we choose to let them be.

Because forgiveness—of others and of yourself—is the only way to tell a new story. To tell a story of victory and triumph and not one defined by hard or even evil moments that may have occurred decades ago. Carrying unforgiveness forces us to live life as victims. When awful things happen to us, we have the choice to stay in the hole dug by whoever or whatever inflicted pain upon us or to crawl out and brush off the dirt. We can decide to let it be. We can put that pain at the foot of Jesus over and over, 490 times if we need to, and perhaps even let the memory of it be fuel for helping others.

There are other women who will be subjected to the same heartache as what you went through, and your experience, your tragedy, may very well be the only thing that helps them. Maybe they won't have to hurt for so long or as hopelessly after they hear your story and see how you have emerged from your hole. You might hold the lighter that can ignite the healing for another person. Your tragedy is that lighter fluid.

I think the Enemy loves when we get stuck carrying the weight of unforgiveness. It must make him very happy to see that big heavy box prevent us from living our lives to their fullest capabilities. He hates—I mean hates—to see us set ourselves free from bitterness and resentment and shame. He probably also hates my prolific use of metaphors. So let's throw in one more.

I'm sure you've heard some variation of the saying, "Resentment is like drinking poison and then hoping it will kill your enemies." I'd like to swap out the word *resentment* for *unforgiveness*. The weight of our unforgiveness only harms ourselves. I don't know about you, but I'm entering the best half of my life and I don't want to carry that poison around anymore. So let's put down that box and walk on feeling lighter. It is, after all, difficult to fluff your throw pillows when your hands are full.

Eighteen

The Ripple Effect (Not the Ones on Your Thighs)

Model Midlife for Others and Define Your Legacy

I want to leave a huge legacy. And I'm not talking about some big fat pile of cash, because let's be very clear: Much to the dismay of my children, I intend to spend every last dime prior to my death. Probably on throw pillows. The legacy I want to leave far surpasses that of finances or properties or antique dishes. I want to leave one that will lift other women, who will in turn lift even more women, and I don't want to create that legacy alone.

Together I want us to rewrite the way women think of life after the midlife point. I believe WE can redraft the script on what it is to fully live during our second half of life. Our legacies, our stories, and our loves can cause beautiful, big ripple effects as far as the eyes can see. It'll be like thousands upon thousands of rocks were thrown into glasslike water and one by one, they ignite the widening circles of a ripple, which only gets larger and larger the farther away it moves from the stone's moment of impact. And as each one's circles expand and devour more of the water's space, they begin to bump into the outer edges of another woman's glorious ripples, and they all grow and grow until suddenly, that once-calm glassy water is wild with activity and motion.

I'm not sure if we've done the damage ourselves listening to generations before us or if it's the ramblings of social media and society, but we are a huge group that for the most part has become silent during a time when we are profoundly needed in this world. I'm pretty sure God never intended for us to become wallflowers watching the hours and days and years tick by. He wants us to be like Lady Godiva riding our stallions through the village, passionate for a cause (not necessarily naked . . . but maybe). Because if we're not dead, God is not done with us.

This is not our time to stop being wild participants of life and just become mere spectators. In fact, I believe exactly the opposite: It's time for us to lead. Yes, lead. Get out there and model for the younger generations what it means to be vibrant women in the second half, what it means to age as God intended. We need to speak up and share our wisdom and help to love and guide those coming behind us.

Let me explain why you are so qualified to lead and to leave giant legacies in your wake.

According to Malcolm Gladwell, ten thousand hours is the magic number for greatness. Spend ten thousand hours practicing a skill, and you will achieve the level of mastery associated with being a world-class expert—in anything.[10] By my calculations, no matter what her career or lack thereof, the average forty-year-old woman has spent at least ten hours a week (two hours a day) doing things like working, being a wife, a friend, a mother, a volunteer, praying, and so much more. Therefore, she has over ten thousand hours in any of those areas and she is an expert.

Now, if so many of us are experts in so many areas, why on earth are we listening to the ones with little to no experience? Why have we chosen this time to be more pulled back and quieter than before? We have the most experience, and yet we are handing the microphone to the people with the least experience. Worse than that, we're not listening to each other, to the voices of our own generation, when we have more to offer each other than ever before. That makes no sense at all.

When did we cross that invisible line of midlife and start using our voices less and less? We were in that center ring for a while, microphone in our hands, and then one day we left the ring. Not permanently, of course; "We'll be right back," we said. We're just going to go have a baby real quick, or get married, or spend a few more years in this mediocre job because the commute is great. The next thing we knew, we were a little hesitant to get back in that ring. Instead, we took a seat on the fifth row and then the twelfth, and one day we looked around and realized that we'd gone from being in the middle of the ring to standing against the very back wall of the audience section. What happened?

I'll tell you what happened: Somewhere in those moments of your kids vomiting red Kool-Aid on your white sofas and trying to fit your slightly expanding hips into two-sizes-too-small shapewear, you started telling yourself the world didn't want to hear from you. You handed the bullhorn over to a young woman who doesn't know the difference between a freckle and an age spot, and now she's telling us we should all wear leggings as pants with short tops. Houston, we have a problem.

We are supposed to work together, we are supposed to have a voice WITH the youth of the world—it's not an either/or situation. Who else is going to explain that those leggings would be much better with a jacket or tunic that hits just below the butt cheeks? This doesn't just give leggings a better name but also hides the evidence of twenty-five years of salt-and-vinegar chips. Are leggings great? Yes. Are they worn in different ways for different ages? Yes. At fifteen they are pants, at fifty-five they are an accessory. I say this as someone who has spent ten thousand hours in leggings.

God doesn't give us years of experiences and lessons for us to be silent about them. It is the exact opposite of what He calls us to do. The Bible says, "Wisdom belongs to the aged, and understanding to the old" (Job 12:12). Just to be clear, *we* are the proverbial "aged" here. That's US! He is saying that *we* are wise, so why would He want us to be the most silent? He doesn't. This, right now, this is the most important time to insert ourselves into opportunities to speak up and lead—at church, in teaching, at work, in community, life groups, friendships, everywhere. We are to use the lessons of our past to share with others.

The world needs your passion, your ideas, your tenacity, and your spark. All of it is YOUR legacy and the start of your own giant ripple effect. But you must decide what your legacy is going to be; no one can decide that for you. All I am here to do is tell you that *we need you to create yours*, to speak up and be on purpose about what you put back into the world right now.

For me, deciding I wanted a legacy was half the battle. Honestly, I'd never given it much thought outside of what throw pillows would go to each daughter. I mean, I suppose I knew what I wanted for my family, like health, happiness, and financial security. But it was a revelation to start considering where else I could leave a legacy, where else I could cause a wee bit of a ripple effect. Who was in my life that I could have a positive impact on other than my family? Luckily, I didn't have to search far.

Take the remarkable Melissa Shoemaker, who runs the operations of everything my company does. I hired her because I'd seen a glimpse of her immense talents when we led life groups together through the years, and I wanted to provide a job that would nurture her gifts and enable her to have a greater impact on the world.

Let me tell you, God placed a giant hand on that woman. He highly anointed her in so many areas. When she is in a room of women, the spiritual knowledge and wisdom that pours out of her blow us away. People come to our retreats excited to meet me, but they leave elated to have met Melissa. Watching her work in a way that makes her soul sing out loud and blesses others is a gift to me.

I also wanted to honor her as a mother. Melissa has three small children at home, one of whom has special needs (which inspired us to create a retreat specifically for mothers of children with special needs).

My goal was to give Melissa space to fully flourish in all that she was, which meant honoring her financially, with my words, and in the tasks I asked of her. Making Melissa part of my team will forever be part of my legacy. I have the opportunity to play a role in what God is calling her to do.

Sometimes all it takes is having one person in your corner allowing you to nurture your giftings, a small part of your world cheering you on saying, "We need you, and your gifts are amazing."

Sometimes the start of those ripples is right in front of you, and sometimes you have no idea what small things you're doing today will ripple into a beautiful story years from now.

One of my favorite stories about leaving such an unintentional legacy has to do with my best friend Kali's house. Many years ago Kali's parents, Kate and Dave, bought a piece of land on Pensacola Beach. It was a beautiful lot with a clear view of the crystal-blue waters of the Gulf. They took months upon months planning every detail of their new home. They focused on quality and built it to resist the wildest of hurricanes with steel pilings and windows that could stand up against a fit of rage from the Hulk himself. It was to be their forever home.

Well, as it turned out, it was not quite the forever home they thought it would be. In 2004, the year they finished building their home, the real estate market was booming. Before they even celebrated their first anniversary in their new home, a stranger knocked on their door and made them a generous offer—actually it was more of a mind-blowing offer—on their home. As luck would have it, five doors down, a friend of theirs was selling their home, and Kate and Dave decided to sell to the overzealous stranger and purchase their friend's house. It was a wonderful and lucrative story.

Then, a few years later, their daughter Kali and her husband, Josh, made a decision to move from Memphis back to Pensacola Beach with their toddler, Braeden. They rented a wonderful condo a mile away from Kate and Dave and shortly thereafter gave birth to their second child, Madelyn. With baby number two, they began to outgrow their little condo and started looking for a house. Well, guess what happened? No really, guess.

Yes! (You're so smart.) The original house Kate and Dave built went on the market (for a less-than-mind-blowing amount), and Kali and Josh bought it. Kate and Dave never dreamed that the home they had put so much love, time, and effort into would be the very place their grandchildren would be raised. That "forever home that wasn't so forever" turned out to be a forever legacy.

Our legacy is not just made up of the things we do, but also of the things we didn't do. What if Kate and Dave had decided to cut corners because "no one would notice"? What would become of their daughter and grandchildren when the hurricanes and tropical storms hit? Or what if I had chosen to underpay Melissa or assign her roles that didn't tap into her strengths? She might have to get a different job, rather than having the time and encouragement to fully be the mother she wants to be and to explore and grow her gifts. My seemingly small decisions of pay and flexible working hours impact Melissa's future, the future of her children, and the future of every woman who is blessed by their time with Melissa at our retreats.

Sometimes the legacy is right in front of us with our children, sometimes it's happening among those we work with, and sometimes it's the unanticipated ones created by our own good works (like we saw with Kate and Dave). But other times, and maybe even most of the time, there are ripple effects that reach across space and time without our knowledge—which is what happened with my friend Andrea and me.

As I've shared with you, I had a hard time admitting that I was even in this mighty midlife stage. What made it even harder for me was that there seemed to be very few women over forty-five acknowledging this slump and even fewer talking about how to navigate out of it. But one of my greatest turning points came in the form of a linen shirt.

While in the midst of my poor-pitiful-me season, my sister Jodie came to visit. She brought with her one of the most fabulous white linen shirts I'd ever seen. It was oversized and flowy and yet it still fit. It was cut to have this easy breezy look to it and I loved everything about it. I immediately went to the brand's website, andandrea.com, and subscribed to their email list. Now, what I am about to tell you is going to make all of you e-commerce and email-marketing people of the world stand up and slow-clap with tears of joy in your eyes: Their welcome email changed my life. No seriously, here's what happened.

After I signed up, I received a series of three separate emails sprinkled over a ten-day period or so. They told the story of Andrea Tonkin, a woman with a passion for design who had put those passions on the back burner while she was married and raising her children. All of it was wonderful, but it was these words that stood out to me:

"Although Andrea's love for fashion remained a 'sideline' during her early years of commitment to mothering and teaching, an upcoming pivotal event (her youngest son finishing high school in 2011), awakened her inner voice. It was shouting! 'What are you going to do in two years after Riley leaves school? How are you going to fulfill your true passion? How are you going to maximize your "Joy" throughout the rest of your life?' At this point, Andrea had no idea what was ahead.

"With a searching heart and open mind, Andrea began paying greater attention to her intuition. Her first 'Aha Moment' came one day by chance. While prepping dinner with the television on in the background, Andrea overheard Oprah chatting with Joan Anderson, the author of *A Year by the Sea*. Joan was describing how she'd devoted her life to her husband and two sons. In doing so, she felt like she'd lost her sense of identity and was committed to making positive changes for her future years. This resonated with and inspired Andrea. She didn't want to get to seventy or eighty years of age and say . . . 'I wish I had.'"[11]

As I read that email describing her story of struggle and triumph, I thought, *A woman in Australia felt the same as I do right now.*

And not only that, an author named Joan Anderson felt that way too.

Joan's story affected Andrea, and Andrea's story affected me. I saw myself in their words; I resonated with them. I felt like these women I didn't know had grabbed my hand and said, "Come here, friend, sit down. Let's talk." In the strangest way, these women, Joan and Andrea, gave me permission to fully chase life as wildly today and with as much impassioned enthusiasm as I had in my twenties and thirties—maybe just a little slower. The action and behaviors of Andrea and Joan were permission slips for me to recognize how valid and universal my feelings were.

Crucially, they were part of planting the seed of what would become this book.

I was changed because they spoke up, they were vulnerable, and they shared their story. The ripple effect of hearing of their struggles and successes affected me deeply. One woman really can change the trajectory of another woman's life simply by sharing her story.

My legacy doesn't begin and end with bringing Melissa on board and adding a throw pillow clause to my will. I am constantly contemplating what ripples I want to make. In what ways can I stir up the water; in what ways can I harness the ten-thousand-plus hours I've spent becoming an expert in life and love and relationships? In long conversations, ergonomic flip-flops, and ordering takeout for large groups? How do I take back the microphone and share what I know about humility and confidence and pain and joy? Not only must I ask myself these questions as I make decisions about how to honor and mentor those I work with, but also as I interact with friends, strangers, my children, my grandchildren, and the wider world around me.

I know that a big part of my legacy comes in my ability to write books and speak publicly, and I do not take that for granted. But I have to remember that the ripple effects of my small decision to not wear a wig during cancer treatments may be equally empowering to another woman struggling with her own hair loss during her treatments. Impacting the life of one single soul has an exponential, unknowable effect.

How about you? As you consider what impact your life is having and will continue to have, remember that legacies and ripple effects can happen in just one small moment or from a lifetime—God uses them both. Perhaps that ripple effect begins with moments with your grandchildren where you whisper in their ears that they are "a mighty child of God." Maybe it's in moments with young coworkers, where you tell them, "You are so gifted, and this world is better for it." Do you know how few times humans have these things spoken over them? Trust me, words create mighty ripple effects.

If you find it difficult to articulate what you want your impact to be, let's go back to the start. Imagine yourself back in the center of that ring, the moments in your life when you felt it all made sense. You were where you should be, you were thriving, you were good at what you were doing, and you knew it. It doesn't matter if that was during your first job shampooing dogs at the local vet, standing in the front of a conference room giving a SWOT analysis to a board of directors, or sitting on the floor with your toddler building a tower of blocks. Is your expertise in graphic design or empathy or PowerPoint or math or defending underdogs or real estate? If you're not still making waves in that area, why not?

This doesn't necessarily mean you have to get another job or lifestyle. It means you should look for opportunities in those areas to contribute, to nurture, to mentor. You have resources and time you didn't have in the past, and my friend, YOU KNOW STUFF. Don't stay quiet about that.

I pray each of ours will be legacies of action and love. From this day forward, may we be on purpose in all our choices, from our words to our connections to our deeds. Let's make sure our voices are heard and our strengths are in use.

I'll end with a story I hold close to my heart, in that place where gratitude and grief about this precious, fragile life quietly coexist. Back in early November of 2021, I received an Instagram direct message from a woman asking about our retreat in April. She explained she had metastatic breast cancer and was still in treatment but would schedule her treatments around attending. She also asked if there was any flexibility in case she needed to rest or eat different foods.

I closed out her message and went to look at her profile, which read: *Kim Hunter, wife, mother, follower of Jesus. In 2012 I was diagnosed with Stage IV breast cancer. Jesus is my healer and strength giver. I embrace wigs! Isaiah 43:19*

It took my breath away. She wasn't just in a cancer battle this year, she was in her *tenth* year. I felt humbled that this little retreat of mine was something she would want to attend. Of course we would make any accommodations she needed.

As the weeks and months passed, our social media chats increased, and I decided that I wanted to personally pick her up from the airport when she arrived. (I usually don't see attendees until the retreat begins.) Kim told me she'd always wanted to see the Gulf, and so, with my dear friends Wendy and Tammy in tow, we headed to the airport to be Kim's personal tour guides.

As soon as we pulled up at the airport, Kim was being wheeled out. She wore a bright pink sweatshirt and pants, white tennis shoes, and a multicolored scarf of pinks, blues, and greens on her head. She was so tiny, almost frail, but when she smiled—wow. You know that phrase "the light of Jesus"? She was that light. She was a small bundle of joyous light and what beamed from the inside of her outshone what you saw on the outside. She was magnificent.

The four of us drove straight to the sugar-white sands of Pensacola Beach, dropping by Kali's beach house for beach chairs and a few hugs. We helped Kim walk across the soft sand. She went straight for the water, which, I might add, was freezing. And just like that, her arms flew in the air and she yelled, "Woohoo!" She slowly twirled and closed her eyes, and her smile seemed to grow and grow.

Watching her in that moment made me want to take stock of all the things in my life. I was witnessing the pure enlightenment of a woman who knows her time on this earth is shorter than she would like it to be. She wanted to soak in every bit of goodness that moment could give her.

That was a month ago. Today, May 13, 2022, I received a call from Kim. Her body was weakening, she told me, and her femur had just broken. She said it was time. As I write this, she has entered into hospice care in Dallas, Texas, surrounded by the love of her husband, Matt, and her children, Hodge and Holt.

I can't begin to know all the ripples that will result from Kim's time on earth, but I do know the impact she had on me and her fellow attendees over the course of our three-day retreat. It was not just the mere power of her presence; every word she spoke felt like a life lesson, and every message was so compelling. To listen to a woman talk about the love of Jesus and the joy she had with Him, even in her current circumstances, was a more profound lesson than anything I could ever teach. The joy she poured out in those three days through her actions, her smile, and her words was incredible.

It's important for all of us to remember that our life circumstances don't have to become dire to have significant, transformative effects on others. We need to look around us, wherever we are, and identify how we can begin to set off ripples big and small. If Kim could make such an impact in a few sweet days, what legacy can you leave with the time that lies ahead of you?

Epilogue

Our Battle Cry

*B*ack when the ideas for this book were swirling around in my head, one visual played over and over in my mind, and it became a foundation of sorts of what this book would be about. I envisioned a large, lush, green field filled with women as far as the eyes could see. Some of them were my current friends I saw often, some were from my past, but most I didn't know. As my eyes scanned the grassy field, I could see intimate groups of women gathered in deep conversation while other women flitted from group to group like butterflies on a spring day. I could feel their energy and hear their laughter permeate through the masses, and it looked like a magnificent dance of feminine life. It was a bustling, busy, joy-filled vision . . . but then it changed.

Far off in the distance, one woman had pulled away from the crowd to catch her breath and rest for a moment. But when she did, the Enemy saw his opportunity and whispered a lie in her ear: "You are too old for this lush, grassy field. The world is done with you. Sit down." It was completely untrue, but the Enemy loves to plant the seeds of fear and untruths in our minds at every opportunity.

That woman believed the Enemy's lies and whispers, and she slowly walked over to another woman who was hanging around the edge of the group, and the first woman shared his deceitful tale with her. Then that woman told another friend, and she told another one.

As each of those women around the edge heard and believed those wicked lies, she sat down feeling defeated and even a bit embarrassed that she'd been caught having so much fun with the other women. A false whisper, a lie from the Enemy, stopped those wildly vivacious women from living out loud. It stopped the world from receiving the wisdom and gifts they were putting out into the ether. It stopped the electric buzz, and one by one the women seemed to settle into the grass and blend into the field like chameleons.

In my mind, I sat down too because I heard the whispers telling me I was done; I was too old and no one wanted or needed me anymore.

Then, after a while, I climbed to my knees to see where everyone had gone. What I saw was so frightening and sad that it made me gasp. Every single one of us was now down on the ground. We were still there, we were still alive, but it was as if we had all simultaneously deflated, as if some external force had caused us to wither and wilt into the grass. Sure, many were still chatting and laughing, but quietly now. We had stopped living out loud and it was all from one stupid, tiny lie.

That vision broke my heart and began this battle cry.

I don't know about you, but I don't want to sit down. Okay, sure, I am out of shape and I do opt for a good sit-down more than I should, but make no mistake, I AM NOT DONE. This ol' girl has plenty to give, and you know what? So do YOU.

It's time for us to push back and change the narrative. It's time to get up. If you're like me, it's going to be more of a roll to the side, then you'll get to your knees and grip each knee as you slowly convince your body to unravel and push yourself into a standing position. Because yeah, it takes a little longer to get off the ground these days. But then—it's time to stand tall.

It's time to turn around to our sisters, take one another's hands in ours, and pull each other up off the ground. Then let's stretch our bodies out as far as they can go, raising our hands so high that we can almost touch the sun itself. When we have stretched as tall as giants, we take a deep breath in and yell, at the top of our lungs, "WE ARE HERE!"

We shout it over and over again until the roar is so deafening that the world actually stops spinning for a moment, taking notice of the life coursing through our veins and our almost blindingly bright light. We are here and on fire!

The world needs these women more than you can possibly imagine. Do you hear me? The world needs us!

We have so much to offer. We still have work to do, people to help, and lives to shape. There are new friendships and relationships waiting for us to step into them and adventures begging for us to lead the way. Our families and communities are not done with us, and God certainly is not finished with us.

It's impossible to have rich and vibrant cultures without the wisdom and experiences of older generations; it just doesn't work. If we garnered all the wisdom of life from those in their twenties and thirties, we'd all believe Instagram was real life, we'd think four hours of sleep is enough, and we wouldn't know that thongs are torture devices linked to a male-driven campaign against panty lines. The world would be missing the depth and substance that comes with at least half a century of accrued wisdom. It'd be without all the interesting and worthwhile contributions we can offer through our unique voice, opinions, personalities, and experiences.

Let's leave the baggage and boxes behind us. Let's purposely take a step into this next chapter of life with joy and confidence, knowing we are exactly who we are supposed to be at this time, on this day, in this very moment. We are exactly what He needs us to be for this next season—nothing more, nothing less. We are no surprise to God, and He will use every single bit of what we give Him.

No matter what your story has been in the past, starting right now, you get to write it. You get to make it a great story of triumph or one of sorrow. You can tell the world, "Look at me now. Look how I've come through all of it." Or you can tell a poor-pitiful-me story. Which one will it be? If you're trying to decide between those two, spoiler alert—you will be happier with a story of triumph rather than a story of victimhood. I don't believe you are a victim; I believe you are a magnificent champion and you are here to do mighty things.

We have long passed the days when we need to worry about impressing someone with our high heels or a job title or our chocolate soufflé (although if I ever actually make one of those, you'd better be seriously impressed). We're in a time of life when our exterior may not be everything we hoped it would be, but our interior is so good and so rich that it is almost bursting to come out. It outshines every small disappointment we may have about our outer packaging. What we have is good; it's really, really good, and it can't be wasted, not for a single moment more.

Do not hide anymore. Do not give excuses anymore. We need you, we love you, and we want more of you.

There is a story in the Bible that has popped into my mind the entire time I've been writing this book, and every time it makes me smile. It's the story of Joshua and the walls of Jericho. (Which, as funny full-circle moments go, is the story the book *The Circle Maker* was based around. Remember, that was the book from my first small group.)

In this story from the Old Testament, God gave Joshua this really unusual strategy for defeating the city of Jericho, which had a huge wall around it. He told Joshua to have his army march around the city, outside the wall, once a day for six days. While marching, the soldiers were to play their trumpets as the priests carried the ark of the covenant around the city of Jericho. (God is nothing if not creative.)

But on the seventh day, God told Joshua that the Israelites must march around the walls of Jericho seven more times, this time in a single day. Then the priests were to give one long blast on the rams' horns. When this happened, the Israelites were to shout as loud as they could, and when they did, the walls of Jericho would collapse and the city would be theirs.

And this is exactly what happened. At Joshua's order, the men produced a powerful roar, and Jericho's walls miraculously fell down. After that, it wasn't long before the city was conquered by the Israelite army.

This is the very short Dawn version, but it's an amazing story—or at least a weirdly cool God strategy—from Joshua 6 of the Bible.

When I think of this story, I think of us. I think of us not understanding the power God has placed within us. This is our Battle Cry, a cry for the world to hear us once again, because each of us is a mighty warrior woman. When we stand up again, the walls will come down, and the blessings will flow.

I want to wrap my arms around you for an uncomfortably long hug and tell you that you have done an incredible job so far. I see in you all the hard, messy, difficult things you have done. I see your exhaustion and inertia and uncertainty about this new chapter of life. You have made this world better just because you exist and are here.

I want to tell you that I love you, and that we absolutely need more of you. Because you, my friend, are magnificent. You are the one-and-only you, and the world would be a little less beautiful without you. I know that the years ahead of you are going to be your best years yet if you will let them be. I know that you have so much left in you to give.

As I like to say, we must not enter the gates of heaven with gifts unopened. God will not say to us, "I gave you so many gifts throughout your life; why didn't you open and use them?" This will not be our story. We will skip into heaven joyfully, leaving behind us a decades-long trail of wrapping paper from opening all the gifts He had for us.

Don't sit back anymore. Don't keep your mouth shut a moment longer. You have so many gifts and so much wisdom. You are going to bless so many people in the years to come. What God has waiting for you is more than you can wrap your mind around.

Get ready, sis, because I'm telling you: God's greatest miracles in your life are yet to come.

Acknowledgments

To the little punk who put that survey together—thank you for motivating me into a Midlife Battle Cry and reminding me that God is NOT EVER done with us!

Craig—My lobster and my perfect partner, God bless you for listening to countless versions of parts of this book, as I begged for your opinions and then proceeded to ignore them all. Thank you for loving me for all that I am and even what I am not.

Makenzie and Ellason—May this book (that you will probably not read for many years) remind you that God is never done with you, never EVER. So live big, love deeply, and work hard till the end of your days so you can support your mother in the manner she has become accustomed to. I love you so much!

Mom and Dad—Thank you for being such good neighbors—we haven't had to call the police on y'all even once! Having you two next door is one of the sweetest blessings of my life.

Rosalie—I am equally pleased that I haven't had to call law enforcement on you or that walker. You are easy to live with and love.

Jodie—Your unconditional love and belief never waver. I'm so glad we wrote books simultaneously so we could commiserate over how painless and joyful it is to write. I love you so very much!

Melodye—You are a precious gift. Thank you for loving us and Rosalie so much.

Nanny—Thank you for always believing in me to a ridiculous level and for being my number one hype girl!

Chloe, Kyla, Sawyer, and Sutton—I love you all to the moon and back; you always make me laugh and remind me what life is all about! Landon, you know I love you, too, sweet son-in-love.

For my family, aka the Clampetts—Uncle Darryl, Kathy, Scott, Katie, Carter, Lucas, and Nanny Sue, I love you so much!

Melissa—God gave me a wonderful gift when He brought you into my life. I adore everything about you. Working with you is a blessing, but having you as a precious friend is the cherry on top! It's an honor to be your FROSS . . . more the FR than the OSS.

Kaylee—My sweet friend, thank you for helping us grow DBM and especially showing us Gizoogle. I love your brilliant mind and beautiful, godly heart.

Casie, Wendy, Tammy, Kali, Bridget, Charlotte, and Caroline—Thank you for being my ride-or-die friends through this. I love y'all so much!

Anderson, Katelyn, Carson, and John Hembree—You are officially in the book. You're welcome.

Ashley Cochrane—You are a photographic genius! Thank you for the fabulous cover and a million other shots that make me look much better than I really do.

To my glorious saint of a literary agent, Claudia Cross—Look, TWO BOOKS! Thank you for being a part of both of them and for being my brilliant champion. Here's to many more!

My team at W Publishing—I loved you from our very first Zoom, and still do! Thank you so much for all of your hard work on this book. You are a magnificent, brilliant, and, best of all, FUN team.

Shari Shallard—You are my writing soulmate. Thank you for turning my piles of literary poop into something beautiful, but especially for knowing big words. You have become a sweet and dear friend to me, and I hope we get to do this together forever. And let me fully acknowledge that if it weren't for that punk and YOU, there would be no book. You are incredible, Shari Shallard!

About the Author

Dawn Barton is a former Olympic curling champion and the face of many *Sports Illustrated Swimsuit Issues*. After successful careers in curling and modeling, Dawn found a passion for the didgeridoo. When she is not in Alaska training to compete in the Iditarod with her dogs, Skye and Birdie, Dawn teaches the didgeridoo to children around the world. She is also a highly accomplished culinary master and a recipient of the Fields Medal, a prestigious award in the field of mathematics.

Most of all, Dawn enjoys a good laugh. None of the above accolades are real, other than the names of her dogs. In real life Dawn is an author, speaker, podcast host of *Porch Ramblings with Dawn Barton*, and the founder of the Retreats at Trinity. She's living the Sandwich Generation dream with her husband, daughter, parents, mother-in-law, and too many animals to count in Cantonment, Florida.

Notes

1. N. J. Falk, "How to Harness the Untapped Spending Power of the 50-ish Super Consumer," *Forbes*, August 21, 2018, https://www.forbes.com/sites/njgoldston/2018/08/21/how-to-harness-the-untapped-spending-power-of-the-50-ish-super-consumer/?sh=1db5d93416db.

2. Andrew W. Roberts et al., "The Population 65 Years and Older in the United States: 2016," American Community Survey Reports, October 2018, https://www.census.gov/content/dam/Census/library/publications/2018/acs/ACS-38.pdf; "2019 Profile of Older Americans," Administration for Community Living, May 2020, https://acl.gov/sites/default/files/Aging%20and%20Disability%20in%20America/2019ProfileOlderAmericans508.pdf.

3. Matthew S. Schwartz, "The World's Oldest Person, Japan's Kane Tanaka," NPR News, April 25, 2022, https://www.npr.org/2022/04/25/1094630648/the-worlds-oldest-person-japans-kane-tanaka-dies-at-age-119.

4. Kenneth Terrell, "Americans 50 and Older Would Be World's Third-Largest Economy, AARP Study Finds," AARP, December 19, 2019, https://www.aarp.org/politics-society/advocacy/info-2019/older-americans-economic-impact-growth.html.

5. Ashley Martina, "My Thoughts on Mental Health Awareness Month," *Ama La Vida* (blog), May 30, 2019, https://alvcoaching.com/blog/mental-health-awareness-month/.

6. "Major Depression," National Institute of Mental Health, accessed August 20, 2022, https://www.nimh.nih.gov/health/statistics/major-depression.

7. Brené Brown, *Daring Greatly: How the Courage to Be Vulnerable Transforms the Way We Live, Love, Parent, and Lead* (NY: Avery, 2012), 45.

8. Glennon Doyle, contributor, "Don't Carpe Diem," The Blog, Huffpost, updated August 1, 2013, https://www.huffpost.com/entry/dont-carpe-diem_b_1206346.

9. "Family Matters: Multigenerational Living Is on the Rise and Here to Stay," Generations United, accessed August 20, 2022, https://www.gu.org/resources/multigenerational-families/.

10. Malcolm Gladwell, *Outliers: The Story of Success* (NY: Little, Brown and Co., 2008).

11. "Discover Andrea's Story," andAndrea.com, accessed August 20, 2022, https://andandrea.com/pages/discover-andreas-story.